DON'T FORGET TO SAY THANK YOU

"Every mom needs the voice of reason and sanity, but we also need someone to point us to God and his generosity. Lindsay Schlegel beautifully combines a deep devotion and realistic humor in this book. You'll feel like she's sitting beside you with coffee (or maybe a beer) even as you want to take notes in the margin. Enjoy this book. And then share it with a friend or three."

Sarah A. Reinhard
Coeditor of *The Catholic Mom's Prayer Companion*
and blogger at SnoringScholar.com

"*Don't Forget to Say Thank You* is a must-have for parents that beautifully and sometimes humorously reveals the many opportunities we have to grow in holiness in the parenting trenches. Schlegel's down-to-earth stories and wisdom reveal the valuable lessons our children impart upon us in between cups of reheated coffee and our constant reminders to be nice, to please go to bed (*now!*), and to say you're sorry. Find encouragement, a new perspective, and renewed strength in your parenting life with this gem of a book."

Kate Wicker
Author of *Getting Past Perfect*

"An inspiration and a challenge to all of us. A gift."
From the foreword by **Danielle Bean**
Brand manager of *CatholicMom.com*

Don't Forget to Say Thank You

AND OTHER PARENTING LESSONS THAT BROUGHT ME CLOSER TO GOD

LINDSAY SCHLEGEL

AVE MARIA PRESS AVE Notre Dame, Indiana

© 2018 by Lindsay Schlegel

Founded in 1865, Ave Maria Press is a ministry of the United States Province of Holy Cross.

www.avemariapress.com

Paperback: ISBN-13 978-1-59471-809-0

E-book: ISBN-13 978-1-59471-810-6

Cover image © RuthBlack/iStock.

Cover and text design by Brianna Dombo.

Printed and bound in the United States of America.

Library of Congress Cataloging-in-Publication Data is available.

FOR JOHN, JACOB, ETHAN, HENRY,
SARAH, AND THOMAS

AMDG

CONTENTS

FOREWORD

BY DANIELLE BEAN

"Be careful!" I called after my twenty-year-old son last summer as he waved goodbye and set out on a grown-up adventure. He was boarding a flight for Tel Aviv, Israel, and I could not help but feel that a piece of my heart was boarding it along with him.

"I will!" he called back with a smile, generously choosing not to roll his eyes until he was out of sight.

But even I rolled my eyes just a bit at my "mom-ness" in the moment. My son was embarking on a personal pilgrimage to the Holy Land, something for which he had saved and planned for many months. He was excited and ready to take on the new adventures that lay ahead. What can a mother's caution to be careful even mean under these circumstances, anyway?

And yet we moms need to say these things. Somehow, we know that our children need to hear them too. Over the years, I've said "be careful" to my children thousands of times, under all varieties of circumstances.

"Be careful!" when, as toddlers, they cracked eggs to add to the pancake batter.

"Be careful!" when they rode a bike for the first time and prepared to let go.

"Be careful!" when years later, they jingled car keys and planned a trip to the beach with friends.

I don't expect the simple words "be careful" to accomplish much in the way of practically preventing my children from making all manner of imprudent decisions. Goodness knows, a shouted "be careful" or not, we've had our share of those.

But a mother's "be careful" conveys so much more than the immediate meaning of those two words alone.

It means, "I love you more than anything and want what is best for you."

It means, "Remember your dignity and worth, and respect the same in others."

It means, "Take good care of yourself out of respect for those who have sacrificed for your health and well-being."

I knew the deeper meaning years ago when my mother said those words to me (and when she still says them!), and I am confident my children know it now.

We moms are often the communicators in our families. As the resident "talkers" in our homes, we say so much more than just "be careful." We also say things such as "stop whining," "go to bed," "eat your dinner," "it's okay," "be nice," and "don't forget to say 'thank you.'"

Just like "be careful," each of these small phrases has a deeper meaning. They communicate important truths and life principles we want to pass on to our children in order to help them become the happy and holy people God wants them to be.

Even if our kids might roll their eyes sometimes, and even if we run the risk of becoming a cliché with our rules and reminders, the true meaning behind the words we repeat, and what we ultimately want to teach our children, is worth reflecting on and explaining to them (and to ourselves) on occasion.

And that is why I am so grateful that Lindsay Schlegel has taken the time to do just that in the chapters you are about to read. With humility and humor, she shares her thoughts about the deeper meaning behind the kinds of things mothers say to their children every day.

St. John Paul II once said that family life is meant to be a "school of love," a place where we learn what it means to love and to be loved by working, sacrificing, and growing up together. The stories Schlegel shares from her own family life and her personal parenting struggles are a real-life playing out of that kind of family living. Each chapter is a peek inside the windows of Schlegel's family as a school of love.

As we read what she shares, it becomes clear that real work toward holiness does not usually happen in flashy, exciting moments. It happens in the everyday living out of our vocations, in relationship with one another. Real love is not always flashy or exciting, either. Real love runs deep in the everyday moments of the ordinary gift of an ordinary day. Truth and love, the real meaning and purpose of our lives, are hidden behind the ordinary things we do and in the ordinary words we say as we grow together inside of a family.

Lindsay Schlegel's sharing of what that kind of love looks like and sounds like in the heart of her home and family is an inspiration and a challenge to the rest of us. As you read this gift of a book, open your heart! Listen to the words you hear and say every day with new ears. Hear in them the unique plan God has for you and your family: a plan for great love that leads to lasting joy.

Acknowledgments

First and foremost, thanks be to God for his creation, mercy, love, and many tremendous gifts in this life and the promise of eternal life hereafter. I am grateful for the graces he continues to bestow on me; the courage to act on them, especially when I find myself in new territory; and forgiveness when I fall short of loving as he loves. I am thankful for the vocation by which he calls me to himself and for my family, the people he set in my path to bring this calling to fruition.

I am enormously grateful to the incredible team at Ave Maria Press for their hard work in bringing this book to life. Thanks to Lisa Hendey for seeing something in these pages and to Amber Elder for making them shine. A big thank you also goes to Stephanie Sibal, Heather Glenn, Brianna Dombo, Jared Dees, Karey Circosta, and Kay Luther, among others.

Thank you to those who have encouraged my writing: my writers' group, the Park Slope Creative Writing Workshop; my teachers from preschool to college; friends who read my first blog, *Young Married Mom*, and saw something in it; the wonderful women at *Verily* with whom I worked as a contributor (especially Krizia Liquido), who gave me a shot and helped me grow; my coworker-turned-friend-turned-editor-turned-agent,

Alexandra Penfold; and Allan Wright, who gave these pages the first thumbs-up and has been cheering me on ever since.

I am grateful to my family for their love and confidence in me. My parents have always believed in me, and my mom gave me the great gift of knowing God as my Father—thank you. My in-laws are true family, and I have learned so much about living the faith with joy by witnessing their example. I am also grateful for the love and prayers of the St. Vincent de Paul parish for my family and me.

John—my blessing, my rock, my love. You are the other half of me and the greatest gift in my life. I understand why you're number one on Jacob's list. You've got the same slot in my heart. Thank you for your humble love and service for me and for our kids. I love you.

INTRODUCTION

I HONOR YOU FOR BEING
A DAUGHTER OF GOD

Growing up, my husband's family had a tradition of honoring each member on his or her baptismal day, the anniversary of that person's being received into the Church. After dinner, everyone said something he or she admired about the honoree. I was introduced to this tradition shortly after John and I started dating and quickly noticed a pattern among his younger siblings.

There was an unspoken rule of no repeat commentary. One phrase came up every time, and there seemed to be a race to get to it first: "I honor you for being a daughter (or son) of God." It was simple, it applied to everyone, it required the least amount of creativity, and it let you get back to your dessert as soon as possible. Despite seeming generic, it was understood to be the most important thing anyone said on a given evening. I didn't get it.

Years later, John and I were married and preparing for the Baptism of our first child. Jacob was a beautiful baby—chunky, content, and cathartic to behold. It seemed to us, as doting new parents, that everyone loved our precious boy. We lived in

Brooklyn and walked everywhere, so I had a fair sense of popular opinion in this regard.

Still, I knew he was going to grow up. At some point, he'd probably disobey me and tell me he hated me. There were likely to be moments when I got frustrated with character traits I had yet to discover. But in those first days and weeks, he was new and fresh and so beautifully alive. I wanted to freeze those moments in my mind, bolt them to my heart so I could raise him with them as my guide. I wanted to form him in a way that honored how special he was even before he could say or do much of anything.

I wanted to honor him for being a son of God.

Really that's what people on the street were doing when they smiled at him, what I was doing when I watched him nursing peacefully, and what my parents did when they came over and we entertained ourselves by watching him wiggle on the play mat.

How was it that everyone could agree that this baby was pure gift but not see the same in each other? All of us were babies at some point, all of us created with purpose, even those whose childhoods weren't quite so sweet. At what point would people stop smiling at Jacob just because he existed and start focusing on his faults? Worse, when would they begin to look right past him, onto the next thing?

I realized there was nothing stopping me from continuing to see the preciousness of life in others, even in myself, if I chose to. It's something we tend to forget over time as we sin and fail and struggle to get back up again. But it's always there. It's a reality without limit, something that, in every interaction, every day, we choose to accept or deny.

• • • • • • • • • • • • • • • • • •

Jacob is seven now, and I have three more children on earth and one in heaven. Each day, I have myriad opportunities to choose whether to act in a way that honors these little ones as children of God. Sometimes I succeed. Too often, I fear, I fail.

As a mother of young children, I repeat the same phrases so many times, they seem to have lost their meaning: "Be patient." "Stop whining." "You need to apologize." And so on.

It was in the midst of uttering these words for the millionth time—and at a greater volume than necessary—that I cried out to God in my heart, frustrated, asking why I wasn't doing a better job of this whole parenting thing. I begged him to explain why he had made me a mother at all. Clearly, I don't have the right stuff. I want to be eternally calm, to discipline my children with gentle firmness, and to not get so angry about the wet towels left on the couch that I forget the totally unique, never-repeatable gift each one of my children is. But then life happens, and I find myself physically tired, mentally wiped, and emotionally at the end of my rope.

Enter the Holy Spirit. There was nothing unique about that moment or that day, except that I was finally ready to listen to someone other than myself. It struck me that I needed to give heed to the words coming out of my own mouth. Maybe I needed to be patient, to stop whining, and to apologize for losing my cool. I had been so focused on my job as a mother—giving directions, making corrections, and looking out for the consequences of my kids' actions—that I had forgotten my identity as a daughter of God. I'd been neglecting the truth of why and how I was created to live in this world.

When I stopped reacting and started reflecting, I was humbled to consider how often in the course of a single day I whined internally rather than offering up my suffering for someone in need. How many times had God asked me to listen to his voice and I chose to direct my attention toward something else instead? How deeply did I appreciate the mystery of daily Eucharist, the ultimate thanksgiving, or was I going through the motions of the Mass, distracted by a hundred other things?

My stagnant faith life began to open up. I realized my journey was still in progress; as a human being, I was still in progress. And that's okay. That's how it's supposed to be. Parenting is messy. Life is messy. Becoming a saint—as we are all called to be—is messy. The path is rarely a straight line, and never is it without peaks and valleys. "Do not be afraid," St. John Paul II tells us, "when love requires sacrifice."[1]

I started to think of my vocation as a mother not only as a responsibility to serve my children but also as a lifestyle to which God has called me to draw me closer to himself. In doing so, I started to recognize the graces I'd been longing for. Motherhood is not something God asks me to do alone. I have physical partnership in my husband. John and I receive supernatural graces through the sacrament of Marriage. At any moment I might call on the Communion of Saints for spiritual strength and encouragement. But if I'm not able to see these graces and accept them in the everyday moments of my life, then surely I am going to be frustrated. I wasn't meant to do it this way.

In Isaiah 49:15, we read, "Can a mother forget her infant, be without tenderness for the child of her womb? Even should she forget, I will never forget you." God wants for me what I want for my children, and he loves me the way I love my children—except exponentially more so, not to mention perfectly.

What do I want for my children? Above all, I want them to know they are loved, no matter what. I want them to embrace God's will in their own lives. I want them to choose Christ every day and to have a personal relationship with him. I want them to be happy, but I also want them to have recourse to something bigger than themselves when life challenges them. I want them to be healthy and strong. I want them to be able to say "I'm sorry" when they're wrong. I want them to do good in the world and to be joyful doing it.

God wants these same things in my life, as they ultimately lead to his glory. My motherhood is not separate from my daughterhood. Rather, it is a more precise direction, a road I have been called to take.

For a long time now, our culture has been interested in the idea of whether women can "have it all."[2] Some say yes, women can have it all but not all at once. This seems fair, but before we can answer the question well, we have to define what "all" is. Is it a family, a fulfilling career, a fit body, ownership of a home and car(s), and a comfortable sense of self? In themselves, these can be good things. It could be that God wants all of these dreams for some women. But is that where it's all supposed to end, just having it? Might the more pertinent question be not whether I can have it all but rather, Is all of it what he wants for me?

Ask any parent of multiple children, and they will say that in many ways, their kids are "night and day," total opposites, completely their own people, despite being nurtured in the same environment. I have seen it in my own children from their first moments out of the womb. Jacob slept peacefully for the first week of his life; I described him as the chillest person I'd ever met. He is still fairly calm and happy to sit on the couch and read or work on a project at his desk. Henry, on the other hand, cried so much when he was born that I thought he was in some kind of pain. Turns out, he's just a loud person, full of imagination, creativity, laughter, and classic little-boy fun.

John and I can offer them the same choices, and they will usually make different decisions. They have different motivations, goals, and interests. They have different paths in this life. Each is so beautifully his own person, loving in his own way, and called by God to something unique but likely something different from the other.

Why would I expect, then, that as a daughter of God, I must be called to the same things as another of my sisters in Christ? There are a million ways to be a mother. There isn't a single path to take. My journey, my particular vocation, is as unique as my fingerprint. God called me not as simply another entity in the larger category of "contemporary woman" but as his beloved daughter. It is in this way that I must respond to him, not necessarily doing what everyone else is doing but recognizing his individual call to me.

This means acknowledging that I am fearfully and wonderfully made, that I am created in the image and likeness of God, and that I should strive for perfection and accept God's mercy and grace when I fall short. It means surrendering myself to his will. It means letting myself be taken care of and letting God be in charge. That doesn't let me off any kind of hook. It's a challenge to accept that I don't have control in the midst of a culture that's telling me I do and I should.

True love requires sacrifice. Sometimes this looks like picking up crushed pretzels from the floor and answering the same questions over and over again. But it always goes deeper than that. The crumbs and the interrogations on the dietary habits of gorillas are God-given opportunities to give of myself to my children. They are also ways for me to come nearer to my Father.

I get frustrated with my kids and yell at them for things I know are natural for them to do. I am impatient. I feel out of control. That's exactly why God called me to this life, so that I could lean on him instead of carrying the well-being of my family alone. As a daughter of God, I now see that my Father gives me certain challenges in my relationships with my children. He gives me encouragement in memories of my own upbringing. He gives me the stories of the saints, the wisdom of his word, the graces of the sacraments, the traditions of the faith, and the rhythms of the Church's year, all in a great effort to create a personalized map toward the joy of heaven.

In the familiar words that come out of my own mouth every day, I have found a way to navigate my vocation with fortitude, love, and prayer; a way to draw closer to our Lord through Blessed Mother Mary and the sacraments; and a way to raise holy, happy, joyful children who, God willing, will grow into faithful, confident men and women, inspired to do their own parts to build up the kingdom of God.

As a daughter of God, I am called to holiness, but as a mother, I am not called to the religious life. Silent meditations and hours of solitary contemplation are not how I spend the majority of my time. Rather, my vocation is lived on my feet, in my home, in school and church communities, and in sometimes-monotonous tedium as I guide my children's hearts toward the love of their Father and mine. God speaks here as often as he does in a convent; I need only to develop the ears to hear. In my experience, his voice comes in a whisper rather than the yell I have trouble toning down.

The message is simple but profound: I am loved simply for being who I am, a daughter of God, a unique creation, a joy and a pleasure for my Father to behold.

My hope is that the Holy Spirit will use the reflections in this book to inspire your own meditations on the ways in which you are called to grow in holiness and then help you to respond to them. Each chapter also suggests a member of the Communion of Saints whom you might call on to open yourself to the graces we need to live our vocation as mothers. If you connect with one saint in particular, I encourage you to learn more about him or her and develop a prayerful friendship.

Whether you read these pages individually or with a group, I pray you will rediscover your Father's tremendous love for you and his desire for you to be close to him. Rethinking motherhood as a means to a more authentic spiritual daughterhood has changed the way I see others and myself. We are all—adults, children, and babies alike—children of God, and we all benefit when we treat each other that way. When we trust God as our Father, we work to build his kingdom. God knows the world needs more patience, humility, courage, and love. These can begin with us.

ONE

ON PAYING ATTENTION

HOW MANY TIMES
HAVE I TOLD YOU THIS?

When you are three and five years old, there are certain things that hold greater value for you than the directions your mother is giving. In my sons' experience, these things have mainly to do with rocket ships, fishing, and catching one's imaginary train. On a given weekday morning, there are things I am bound to repeat ad nauseam—make your bed, get dressed, finish your juice, and brush your teeth. Who wants to put on shoes when there's a fire to fight? Why get dressed when the other guy in the room is clearly yearning to be pounced upon and tackled to the ground?

After I say the same thing three or four times, rather than say it again, I'm equally as likely to ask my kids how many times I've repeated myself. My older son, the pragmatist, will offer an accurate account. My younger son is less attached to reality, and I can expect the same answer from him every time: "a hundred and a half." It sure can feel like it.

If you are of as little patience as I am, being ignored is aggravating. Most of the time when I get worked up, the boys remain

unfazed. I wonder why I bother. But I want the best for them.
I want them to be safe and happy. I want them to learn to love
in all things.

Considering the same situation in the context of my relationship with God is humbling, to say the least. I started going
to daily Mass in college and have been a faithful participant,
barring illness and short postpartum recovery periods, for a
dozen years. I hear the Word of God a lot. I serve as a lector and
spend the week leading up to my slot reading and rereading
the text, trying to understand it from the inside out so I can
proclaim it in a way that will, through the wisdom of the Holy
Spirit, move hearts.

Apart from the readings, so much of the Mass itself—the
prayers, the responses, and the hymns—is taken right from
scripture. Daily Mass is a beautiful way to be enveloped in the
Word of God. When I am fully engaged, I delight in the different
voices proclaiming, praying, and responding; in the Hosanna,
when our voices join with those of the angels and saints; and in
the sign of peace, when we offer an act of charity to our neighbors. I think of the places in the world where this isn't possible
on a daily basis, where it's risky to participate in worship at all.
It is an incredible opportunity to have the Mass celebrated just
up the street from my house every single day, without any fear
of danger for going.

And yet how often do I hear the word of my Father during
Mass and ignore it? I hear that I cannot "serve God and mam-
mon" (see Matthew 6:24), but my mind wanders to a work project, and I let it. I hear that I should not worry about what I will
eat or wear—simply look at how the birds or the lilies are cared
for—but I make a mental grocery list anyway. I hear that Jesus
is the way, the truth, and the life, but I spend the time in his

presence overly concerned with the details of my own life. I think through emails I need to send. I reconsider my schedule after Mass and wonder how it's all going to fit in. I hear that I must love my enemies and forgive more times than I can count, but instead I rehash that conversation that upset me and imagine what I should have said. I hear Jesus beg the disciples not to hinder the children from coming to him—no exceptions—and then lose my peacefulness with one of my own children, who is loudly picking the kneeler up and down for what might actually be the seventy-seventh time.

My humanity, my concupiscence, and my self-centeredness get in the way. Most days, I have the spiritual attention span of a goldfish. I am easily distracted from the tremendous supernatural mystery I have the gift of being a part of every day. Given, taking little ones to Mass is rarely a peaceful experience. Someone has to go to the bathroom; someone else drops a hymnal; there is poking and giggling and shouting over who's sitting in whose seat. It would be easy to say these are the reasons I miss what God's trying to tell me. To some extent, it is, and that's okay. But there's more. If I'm honest with myself, it's because I'm not really trying hard enough.

The thing about my boys is that more often than not, they hear what I say. They simply choose not to listen. Hearing is inactive. Listening requires a response. And that response often requires a sacrifice they're not inclined to make. Young children—and let's be honest, many of us adults too—are ruled by their own desires. They change activities on a whim, always excited for something new and novel to entertain them. They haven't yet internalized the paradoxical rewards of putting someone else before yourself. Sometimes I wonder if I really get it yet.

On the rare occasion that I am at Mass alone, I still have trouble paying attention. The length of my nails becomes fascinating as the prayer of consecration I have heard hundreds of times begins yet again. That text I've been meaning to send is suddenly of utmost importance and must be mentally drafted, stat. I can think of a million different things, but I struggle to focus on the mystery, the miracle happening before my very eyes.

When I do manage a glimpse of this, I am consistently awestruck at everything the Mass includes. It is the ultimate prayer. We plead forgiveness, we pray for our neighbors, and we consume the Word of God in the readings and in the Eucharist. As a community, we praise our Lord, recognizing all he is and all he wants for us. This is medicine for the troubles in my life outside the church's walls. This is strength to live my vocation as he intended. This is sustenance for the journey of life. This is everything I'm looking for everywhere else. It is a necessary time away from the things that have a tendency to consume me and divert my attention from my reality as a daughter of God, from the relationship my Father wants to have with me. I was made to love and be loved.

I'm not always excited about going to Mass. It seems too much effort some days, and it feels as if I have too many other things to do. I go through the motions out of habit and with only a vague understanding of what it is I'm doing. I don't make the effort to give my full attention because I'm not totally convinced of what I'm going to get out of it. I still doubt. I still question.

If this is all I'm putting into Mass, it shouldn't be too surprising that I'm not getting much out of it. I cannot earn graces. God pours them out at his will, but I need to be receptive to them if they're going to make a difference.

Mass is not supposed to be a passive endeavor; it is an opportunity to give thanks for the gift of Christ's life on the Cross. It's the spiritual battery power I need to live my life with God as the center. It is time to engage with my community, to profess shared belief, and to encourage each other on the journey to holiness. It means admitting I mess up, which can hurt. It means being honest about not being able to do it all alone and being okay with that, even being joyful because of it. It means sacrificing something of myself to experience the goodness my Father wants for me.

Much of what my boys ignore from my mouth are admonitions to be careful, to not hurt anyone, to take care of each other, and to choose a loving response. My Father wants the same for me. He gives me everything I need to do it. But you can't force someone else to listen to you. Trust me; I've tried.

The repetition of the Mass is not permission to zone out. Rather, it's a reiteration of a message I desperately need to hear. I am a sinner, but I am loved just as I am. Despite what the world tells me, I am enough. The love of Christ is not something I need to earn. I couldn't, even if I tried. But I can choose to respond to it. I can hear, listen, and act. It means I have to give up something of my own, be it pride, time, energy, or the control I think I have over how my life is going to look. It means putting God first.

This is so much easier said than done, both inside and outside of Mass. I hit the snooze button instead of starting the day with purpose and direction. I choose to flip on the television in the evening rather than spend that time in prayer. I worry about the shape of my body or the clothes on my back rather than how to give generously of my blessings to those in need. I lose my cool when the toddler refuses to sleep during a carefully planned nap. I get upset about something related to work and let it manifest as a short fuse with the kids.

Even when my children don't seem to listen to me, even when I run out of patience, I never run out of mercy and love. They can always, always come back to me, no matter what. This is even more powerful when it comes from God. He is infinitely patient; he is patience itself. I can never mess up so much that he won't take me back.

They say misery loves company. When I turn to the scriptures, I see how many people over the centuries have heard God's Word and ignored it for one poor reason or another. Beginning with Adam and Eve, then with the Israelites, and on into today, we find that the things of this world consistently fail to satisfy the basic yearning of the human soul. And yet we continue to look to them for solace from the challenges and heartaches of life.

The good news is that in every situation, God returns to his people with mercy. He knows we're going to mess up. He knows it's going to be a bumpy road, but he never stops offering us opportunities to renew our connection with him.

Modern life can pull me in a thousand different directions, often before I've managed to eat breakfast. The times I am most aware of this is when I am preparing for Confession. I go through the commandments one by one and consider how I have disobeyed them. Oh, let me count the ways! There is always a theme running through my transgressions—I have chosen myself before the other, be it God, my family, or a stranger. I have failed to trust my Father. He gave me the answer, but I didn't really listen. I either thought I knew better or blatantly ignored him and thus put myself and others in danger of one kind or another. God's answer? "I forgive you. Come back to me. Let me show you again what love truly is."

I do the same for my children. After a time-out and a hug, I am often compelled to look my children in the eye and say, "Listen, I love you. This, whatever happened, is going to be fine. We'll try better next time, okay?"

I want them to make good choices, but I also want them to know that their worth does not hinge on what they do or don't do. They are priceless and precious simply because they are children of God. How do I get that through to them? I'm still struggling to understand it myself.

The Mass reminds me. The Confiteor lets me say I'm sorry. The readings give me instruction. The Eucharist gives me the energy to pursue holiness. By listening, by taking it all in, I become more receptive to God's Word and his will for me. When I pay attention, when I give my heart, mind, and will to my Father, I can hear what he's trying to tell me, even if it's for the millionth time.

When I get off track, I don't need to wait for a big moment of revelation to draw closer to our Lord again. It can be tough amid all the responsibilities I have as an adult and as a parent to remember that I am first and foremost a child of God. He wants to spend time with me, converse with me, celebrate with me, and grieve with me. All of this happens in the course of the Mass. His work in me did not end when I became a parent; indeed, parenting is the holy work to which I was called before I drew a single breath.

My kids are prone to blame their distractions on something else, sometimes even each other: "I was reading this." "He was pushing me." "He took that toy." "I wanted to see how this worked." In every situation, I tell them, they have a choice. No one else decides to what they give their attention. There may be temptations, and I may need to help remove them, but the choice of where to look and what to respond to is always, always theirs.

This is advice I need to heed on a deeper level, both to better engage with the Lord and to be a better example to my kids. I can stop reading through news on my phone to spend time in the morning in prayer. I can reject worldly thoughts while I contemplate our Lord and his Blessed Mother in eucharistic adoration and the recitation of the Rosary. I can look through the Mass readings the night before so that I am better prepared to engage with the liturgy and draw on the graces of the Holy Eucharist to sustain me in the day ahead.

I know I will slip up. I will still get distracted. I see my faults, my disobedience, and my refusal of God's love and believe that these things diminish my worth as his daughter. But God doesn't see things that way. He loves me more perfectly than I am able to love my children or myself. His forgiveness is greater than mine; his mercy, more complete. He offers his love anew every day, in every circumstance. This is what I am striving to emulate.

Time and again, God has proven to me that he is trustworthy, love-worthy, every-moment-of-my-day-worthy. And yet just as many times I have chosen to be consumed with something that seems more entertaining, more gratifying, and less costly. I have chosen to fight an imaginary fire rather than respond to the call of the parent who loves me with his whole being.

If I am to live my vocation well, I will dispose myself to hear the voice of my Father. God has seen it all before. And he loves me still. If only I am willing to listen, he is teaching me at Mass and in the ordinary moments of the day how to love my kids in the way that he loves me.

The good news is that even after he's said it a thousand times, he'll say it again and again to draw me back to him: "You are mine. I love you. Follow me."

• • • • • • • • • • • • • • • • • • •

REFLECT

- What do you choose to hear rather than opening yourself up to God's Word? What activities take the place of daily prayer time?
- How can you reorder a moment of your day—morning, afternoon, or evening—to focus on hearing God's Word? What difference do you hope it will make?
- How does contemplating God's patience with you change your perspective on another relationship in your life, be it with a child, your spouse, or another family member or friend?

• • • • • • • • • • • • • • • • • • •

PRAY

God, help me to truly listen to the words you have already spoken so many times to me. Help them to settle into my heart and soul. Give me the grace to love your Word and to put it into action today.

• • • • • • • • • • • • • • • • • • • •

CALL ON THE COMMUNION OF SAINTS

The Bible does not record a single word spoken by St. Joseph, adoptive father of our Lord Jesus Christ. When the angel came to him and asked him to stay with Mary and to care for her and the child Jesus, his silent affirmation helped God's will come to fruition. St. Joseph's parenting depended on listening carefully to his own Father. That faithfulness translated into the courage to respond, for the glory of God.

St. Joseph, pray for us.

TWO

ON OBEDIENCE TO GOD'S WILL

STOP WHINING

For the first few months that they were enrolled in karate lessons, my sons whined every week about donning their uniforms and making the five-minute trek across town. My older guy's class met twice a week, so he whined on Thursdays *and* Saturdays. Their reluctance to stop what they were doing, as well as their uncertainty about what was to come, manifested in tear-filled complaints and attempts at negotiation. "What will I get out of this?" "Don't I know all this already?" "What's the point?" "I'd rather have dinner." The big guy once argued, "I'm not learning what you think I'm learning. I'm only learning the moves, not that thing that starts with *D*!"

But we'd signed up and paid for these lessons, so I stood my ground: they were going. That thing that starts with *D* is discipline, and like it or not, every time they suited up and loaded into the minivan, they learned something of it. No matter the crying and screaming before we arrived at the studio, once they walked in the door and got moving, the kids always enjoyed themselves. They were learning to follow their instructors and to model forms for their juniors. In doing so, they were also learning to care for the bodies God gave them, their little temples of the Holy Spirit.

A few months later, their classes got more challenging. More was being asked of them—more of a time commitment, more focus, and more responsibility to the rest of the class community. They started testing for belt promotions, and having a goal in sight made a tremendous difference. They don't whine anymore.

While they might not put it this way, they are experiencing the peace and fruitfulness of discipline and obedience. There is hope in knowing that all this hard work is leading somewhere. They have found they can trust their teachers and me and that there is good in this process that they couldn't see at the start. They practice all over the house now, teach their little sister the moves they used to think were a waste of energy, and say things like, "I love karate!" And they mean it.

I see in my boys the second son in Jesus' parable about obedience, the man who says he won't follow his father's instructions but eventually changes his mind and does as he was asked (see Matthew 21:28–32). When my kids surrender themselves to the rhythm of the class and the instructions they're given, they find a pleasure and satisfaction they were unable to generate on their own.

Though they don't whine about karate anymore, they do whine about other things—cleaning up, taking a bath, going to bed, and so on. Sometimes I wonder where they learned this behavior. Then I look in the mirror and see my answer staring back. I am no stranger to kicking and screaming when my Father asks me to do something I don't want to do, though my reaction is typically more figurative than literal. I get cranky, sigh a good deal, and ask numerous rhetorical questions that begin with, "Why can't you just . . . ?" I'm an adult, but I still don't like it when things don't go my way or when more is asked of me than I am willing to give. In theory, I want to be obedient to the Lord, but that discipline in practice is a different story.

Just like my children, I fail to see the bigger picture. I'd rather stew in my frustrations than extend forgiveness when I'm hurt. It's easier to judge someone else's misstep than give the person the benefit of the doubt and examine my own conscience. The little things in my life can seem as if they don't have a place in the larger story of salvation. I imagine that to me they are infuriating, but that Jesus doesn't care about them. He's got bigger fish to fry, and my details are insignificant, unimportant. The Cross is one thing; my life is another.

Except that it's not. God uses everything for the good. Discipline and obedience go hand in hand. Both are built on a foundation of trust. When through his grace I choose to be obedient to his call, the discipline I undertake prepares me for further challenges. It strengthens me to choose his will over my own. The more I choose Christ, the less I am tempted to choose myself. "He must increase; I must decrease" (Jn 3:30).

Advent and Lent are two seasons of intense training in the liturgical calendar that offer a more profound time to stop whining and to grow in discipline and obedience. In my mind, they are similar to training for a road race. I try to exercise regularly throughout the year, but when there's a big running date on my calendar, the weeks leading up to it are devoted to preparation. My whole life is affected—what I eat, how much I sleep, and how much I agree to take on in other areas of my life. I order my life to give all I can to my goal.

So it is with discipline for the soul. Lenten disciplines are more popular, but Advent is also a period of preparation. Both give us the opportunity to refocus our hearts on the Lord, shed the attachments that interfere with a close relationship with him, and open our ears to hear his voice more clearly. These purple-robed seasons are times in which we relearn discipline and obedience. We relearn how to trust in the Lord.

The power of obedience and the uselessness of whining occurred to me in a powerful way during the Triduum the year my daughter was born. Having a newborn similarly causes the lesser elements of life to come to a halt. In the hours spent holding and nursing my baby, I must be still. Looking into her face, I know that the Lord is God.

Sarah was born on a Sunday during Lent. The Friday before her due date, I went to my parish's evening Stations of the Cross, in large part because I hoped the fourteen genuflections would start labor. It took a day or so to take effect, but it worked. Rather than watch the season finale of *Downton Abbey* that weekend, my husband and I booked it down a major highway in snow and slush, barely making it to the hospital before our little girl was born into the world. We now had a delightful dash of pink and peach tones in loads of laundry otherwise dominated by shirts emblazoned with trucks and pajamas with glow-in-the-dark dinosaur bones.

A few weeks later, Good Friday was an appropriately gray and dreary day. Because we go to morning Mass every other day of the year, Holy Thursday, Good Friday, and Holy Saturday always feel different in a powerful way. I don't really know where to start our day. There's something missing, something lost from our routine, something I quickly want to find again.

I took Sarah for a walk that morning. There is a section of our town generously termed "downtown" in the half mile between our house and the church. It was completely still as I passed back and forth through it. The baby was quiet from the motion, and I absorbed the sense of stillness rendered by the day.

I wondered if I'd done enough that year for Lent. With being pregnant and giving birth, the season had had a different rhythm for me than it had in the past. But like so many times before, I felt like I hadn't given enough. Too late, I realized I'd wanted to offer more. I wasn't sure I'd sacrificed enough to yield that sense of release and relief at Mass on Easter morning. I thought, as I had in years past, that I was kind of bad at Lent.

I returned home from the misty walk to find my husband taking the boys, then two and four, out for a bike ride, enjoying the day off of work before the afternoon service at church. The house was quiet. I took Sarah to the rocker in her room to nurse, and she fell asleep in my arms. The stillness probed further into me.

For the first time that Lent, I seriously meditated on the fact that Christ died on the Cross for our sins. A man died. The mysterious Incarnation of God in human flesh gave up all else that he might have done or been in this world to save us—to save me—from sin. And he did it because his Father asked him to. He didn't whine. He didn't complain. When God did not choose to take Jesus' cup away from him, he stood as tall as he could muster after being brutally beaten and walked the road set before him.

It occurred to me that I was not living in a way that honored that. I went to Mass daily and I went to Confession somewhat regularly. I trusted in the Church's wisdom and tried to allow it to guide my life. But if I was honest with myself—as I was in this moment—I went through most days only nominally aware of Christ's sacrifice. Rarely did I seek an opportunity to let the gravity of my faith settle into my bones. I moved too quickly. Some of my disciplines had become habits I performed without considering their deeper meaning. My obedience crumbled before my will. I was spouting off my thoughts in prayer, but I hadn't listened to God's reply in much too long. I saw now that if I could better internalize the truth of Jesus' death, and not just rejoice in his resurrection, I would be a different woman, a better mother, and a closer follower of Christ.

I rocked in the silence that day, truly feeling as if someone I loved had died. It hurt, and I felt sad and helpless. There was nothing I could do about it.

Well, there was nothing I could do to go back and undo it. But there was something I could do about it now: I could submit myself more fully to God's will, trust him more completely, doing as Jesus did, and putting my life in his hands. This one day felt more powerful than the previous forty. I'd stopped making Lent about me and had surrendered my will to his.

There's a lot of junk on the internet, but one Twitterism that I find worthwhile is #firstworldproblems. I've come to use it in casual conversation as there are a lot of things I could, and do, get frustrated about in my daily life. Little things, like that sippy cup that isn't actually spill-proof or that snack cup lid that only keeps the food contained until your child learns to remove it altogether. Then there are the temper tantrums about cleaning up, that third desperately needed sip of water before bed, and the stomach flu that takes the family down one at a time, obliterating everything on the calendar for a fortnight.

None of these things is ideal, but they all really are first-world problems. My kids have food. I have the support of my family, school, and church communities in raising my kids. We have more books than I care to count. Everyone has a bed in our cozy house. We have access to health care and insurance to help keep our children healthy and strong. How often do I give real thanks for these things? Instead, I complain about the little things that are driving me up the wall.

Really, it's not the sippy cup or the tantrum that upsets me. It's the interference with the plan I had for myself. I don't like it when things don't go my way. I like to be in control. I really, really like it. Intellectually, I know I'm not really in control of anything but myself, but I like to pretend otherwise. In reality, though germs are invisible, they're there. My kids have free will. God has a better plan than mine.

I can't see his plan when I'm whining about the little things and letting them get me down. I can't see past what I want, what I think is important, and what I think everyone else needs. There's no room in my peripheral vision for something more profound, for something mysterious, and for something that might not immediately make sense to me. There isn't room for me to make a sacrifice.

That's not the way Jesus was thinking when he surrendered himself to the Cross.

In his *Spirituality of Waiting*, Fr. Henri Nouwen notes that the verbs used to describe Jesus' passion are passive, rather than active. Fr. Nouwen explains, "Jesus does not simply fulfill his vocation in action, but as much in passion. He doesn't just fulfill his vocation by doing the things the Father sent him to do but also by letting things be done to him, the Father allows to be done to him."[3] He knows he's not in control. He's not trying to be. He trusts his Father. He obeys his Father.

In the same way, I can choose to forgo the plans I have for myself in order to respond to God's call. Instead of trying to manage every moment of my day and every interaction I may have, I can open my heart and my mind and ask the Holy Spirit to help me see what God wants me to see. Where is there a need I can fill? Where can my gifts be used to someone else's benefit? Who needs me to just sit and be with him or her for a little while? How will I respond if this call conflicts with my expectations?

This surrender is as important in the little things as it is in the big things. When I look to Jesus' example, I see that he built up his stores of discipline day by day so that he could put that trust into action in his ultimate sacrifice. Of course he didn't have sin to trip him up, but he did experience human emotions as we do. He did make the choice to commit to discipleship and obedience, both of which bolstered his trust. And because he trusted his Father, because he had given himself over to the Father's will completely, he didn't have anything to whine about—not even death.

I have not had as intense an understanding of that mystery since, but I think of that day when I question how faithful I am being to the Lord, which I should probably do more often. When I reflected on Jesus' passion that Good Friday, I didn't know what it meant for my life yet, but I knew it had to be about more than just that day or just that season. I knew that I was attracted to Jesus' confidence, to his strength in weakness, and to his total gift of self. I knew, too, that these things were not the fruit of whining about the frustrations of my day, however real they may be. Like the second son in the gospel story, and like my boys whining about karate class, I'd been resisting the fullness of God's call, not sure what it would mean and not sure what kind of sacrifice it would require.

I'd spent nearly thirty years of my life not really understanding Jesus' passion. It felt as if I was only scratching the surface now. I had a long way to go. I didn't even know how I was going to be different when the boys got back from their bike ride.

The one thing I did know was that God had used my motherhood to give me the opportunity to sit with him for a little while that day, to wait with him, and to recognize that he is God and I most certainly am not. While I joked that having a baby during Lent meant I now had an excuse to eat cake on a random day in that penitential season each year, God used the same event to set me up to be truly still for an hour or so and experience Good Friday as I never had before.

There's a popular saying that you can't have Easter Sunday without Good Friday. This is an important reminder in a culture that values instant gratification and sees little to no meaning in suffering. Discipline means suffering in some way, even though it's usually not as extreme as being nailed to a cross. Likewise, obedience requires sacrifice. Together, they deepen trust, encourage faith, expand hope, and foster love. Easter Sunday was glorious, but Good Friday was a tremendous act of charity, made possible because Jesus trusted in his Father in thought, word, and action. His integrity, his surrender, is our salvation.

It wasn't too late for the second son in the gospel, and even when I mess up, it's never too late for me to choose to allow God to work in me. I can always choose his path and his truth, even if I have rejected them before. The word *disciple* comes from *discipline*. Being a disciple is about being trained by someone who knows the way.

God knows my heart; he knows my needs. My weaknesses and faults are no surprise to him. Like any good parent, he will wait with the light on until his child comes home.

• • • • • • • • • • • • • • • • • • •

REFLECT

- Have you had an experience of Lent or Advent when you felt you hadn't done enough to prepare? How did that impact your celebration of Easter and Christmas?
- When you are called to grow in holiness, what practices do you take up? Are they things you've chosen on your own, or do you look to prayer or spiritual direction to guide you toward a sacrifice?
- How does your children's understanding of these seasons of preparation influence your own spiritual journey?

• • • • • • • • • • • • • • • • • • •

PRAY

Lord God, at certain times during the year you call me to prepare my heart anew for your coming. Whether or not I am in one of those seasons now, help me to see what you need me to offer up to grow closer to you. Help me to seek pure guidance where it can be found and to do your will, rather than my own.

· · · · · · · · · · · · · · · · · · ·

CALL ON THE COMMUNION OF SAINTS

The Blessed Virgin Mary gave a wholehearted yes to God's will in birthing our Savior. Her consent to conceive a child through the Spirit meant that she could lose her husband and end up alone in a society that didn't always take great care of women. But her trust wasn't in this world; it was in God. By giving up her life here on earth, she gained an eternity in heaven.

Blessed Virgin Mary, pray for us.

THREE

ON ACCEPTING OUR CROSSES

NO ONE SAID IT WOULD BE FAIR

There is little that can outrage a child more than being given less of something than a sibling or classmate. Children come equipped with a sense of fairness that is maddeningly impossible to keep up with. His glass of chocolate milk is fuller. He's had that toy for a long time already. She gets to go to Disney World.

It can be tough for any of us to accept that we just can't have everything we want (even if we listen to that Rolling Stones song "You Can't Always Get What You Want" on loop). It would be great if we could shed this deep-seated sense of injustice as we become adults, but for most of us, that isn't the case. We transfer the complaints to what I'd argue are less exciting things: Their child is more obedient. He works better hours. She's in better shape. But maybe that's because I like chocolate milk too much.

Our culture encourages us to make plans and gauge our success—or worth as human beings—by whether or not we bring them to reality. Too often, I forget how much is out of my control.

As a child, I played house all the time. My friends and I talked about the kind of men we'd marry; how many children we'd have, including the number of boys versus girls; and where we'd live. We were young and innocent and full of dreams. As we grew up, we found that you can't control when you'll meet your spouse. Jobs can dictate where you'll live. And being pregnant doesn't mean you'll bring home a baby.

My husband and I were so excited when we conceived our second child. We wanted a big family. We were young, healthy, and able to support ourselves. We knew we were blessed, and we rejoiced. We went to a nine-week ultrasound and fell in love with a bean with a heartbeat. Three weeks later, I went by myself for another routine scan. John was on a thirteen-hour flight home from a business trip in Hong Kong. There were arms and legs on the screen now, the definite shape of a child. But there wasn't a heartbeat.

While I waited for the doctor to bring me the written report, I heard a voice from somewhere within me gently say, "It wasn't your fault. You didn't do anything wrong." I clung to that in the weeks that followed. I was numb initially, but I knew the grief would hit me. When it did, I couldn't pray. I could barely get myself out of bed to care for then sixteen-month-old Jacob. I felt lost, shattered. At one point, John asked when "old Lindsay" was coming back. I told him I didn't think she was.

It didn't seem fair that I wasn't the woman he'd married anymore and that I wasn't caring for Jacob with the same enthusiasm I used to. I was so empty, so drained. I ached. I cried. Seeing these short, concise words on the page don't do justice to the evenings I spent staring into the patterns of our living room rug, trying to make sense of something, of anything. I needed something to hold on to, or better, something that would buoy me up while the tides of grief rushed over me and I tried to figure out what happened next.

I mourned the passing of this child, Ethan, and was simultaneously desperate to conceive another. I craved the warm weight of a child in my arms, the satisfying release of nursing to nourish a tiny soul. I knew a half dozen other women with due dates within a week of mine. I was not jealous of them; I understood that my child was not meant to live longer than he did. But that didn't lessen the pain. I'd had a child, and now I didn't. How would I answer people when they asked how many children I had?

I feared asking friends how their families were doing. I thought it was a real possibility that someone's two- or three-year-old child had died, but no one had told me. Death could happen anywhere, at any time, to anyone. It was more real to me than it had ever been before. We'd lost our child with no warning, no symptoms. The doctor said Ethan had died two weeks before that ultrasound. I hadn't even known, and I didn't know where to begin processing that.

• • • • • • • • • • • • • • • • • •

Intellectually, I know that I will truly be happy when I give everything in my life up to the Lord. In practice, this is usually a tremendous challenge for me. I like to believe I am in control of how events unfold in my life, rather than only how I'll respond.

But in this case, my handing over the situation to the Lord was barely an act of will. I didn't have that kind of courage in me. I felt like the apostle Peter when Jesus questioned him about his intentions after many other followers had walked away from the Lord. "Master, to whom shall we go?" Peter says. "You have the words of eternal life" (Jn 6:68). Even if I'd wanted to turn somewhere else, I didn't see any other options.

Years before we lost Ethan, I was introduced to St. Ignatius of Loyola's Suscipe prayer in an undergraduate course on Ignatian spirituality. It sounded nice and appealed to my sense of lyricism. My theology professor, however, impressed on our class the radical act of submission it really was.

> Take, Lord, and receive all my liberty, my memory, my understanding and my entire will, all I have and call my own.
>
> You have given all to me. To you, Lord, I return it.
>
> Everything is yours; do with it what you will.
>
> Give me only your love and your grace, that is enough for me.[4]

I trusted it was important and got into the habit of offering it up daily after receiving Communion. I often remembered being told it was a big deal, but I didn't have much opportunity to put it to the test—until I went to that horrible ultrasound.

It wasn't fair that our child died. It's also not fair that John and I have not struggled to conceive him or our other children. It's not fair that we had opportunities that led us to the schools we attended and the jobs we secured. It's not fair that Jacob has life-threatening food allergies. It's not fair that I have the time and space to write this book when other women struggle all day, every day, to try to feed their families. Life isn't fair. But then, I don't recall fairness in that sense being a necessary element of Christian discipleship. Holiness is determined not by which cards you're dealt but by how you choose to play your hand.

I would not have chosen this path for my family, nor would I want to go back in time and have the chance to choose whether or not to lose Ethan. Of course I would have loved to know him, to hold him, and to see him in real life. But if I hadn't lost Ethan, I wouldn't have my Henry. And if I didn't have Henry, I wouldn't have my Sarah. And so on. This is God's will, not mine.

Some days, it's hard to believe the miscarriage happened at all. The ultrasound pictures that I have in my bedroom and the ring engraved with Ethan's name that I wear on my finger remind me that it wasn't all a bad dream. With God's grace, I was able to accept that my second child was never meant to take a breath in my arms or sit at the dinner table with us. I was not meant to bring him home. I was not meant to even be sure if Ethan was a boy.

When it all happened, I was too tired and broken to try to control things myself. I welcomed God in to make sense of the pieces I'd crumbled into. I will never be the same. I was crushed, and some of the cracks are still there. But I became more of who God needs me to be. I know I can trust him. I know I can lean on him. I know he is there for me in the Eucharist, in my husband, in my family, and in my children. I know he will not leave me.

This is not to say there wasn't pain then or that grief doesn't still find me now. January is always a challenging month, since it holds the anniversaries of Ethan's death and the ultrasound. My tears flow in other, seemingly random moments, too, when I'm reading books or watching TV. I drive past a street that bears his name. I look at our other kids and can almost see the gap Ethan left. I write Henry's full name—Henry Ethan Schlegel—on a form and think of this other child, who will never go to kindergarten, who will never grow up. I mourn again—or perhaps, still—when I hear of another family who has lost a child.

St. Paul tells us that "he gave some as apostles, others as prophets, others as evangelists, others as pastors and teachers, to equip the holy ones for the work of ministry, for building up the body of Christ" (Eph 4:11–12). In the same way, God gives some of us the cross of miscarriage. He gives others infertility and still others terminal illness. It is senseless to try to rank these. Who would win—the one with the most trying situation or the one with the easiest ride?

Suffering can be redemptive, and I can say with certainty that the work my child is doing in heaven is nothing short of miraculous. He has drawn me closer to God than anyone else has. In talking and writing about him, I have come to know other women who have lost children to miscarriage and stillbirth and to call them friends. Some of their experiences feel more tragic than mine, but I have to remind myself not to compare. God gives us the crosses he wills for us, and if we ask, he supplies the graces to navigate them as well. It isn't fair, but fair isn't a stop on the road to heaven.

As an adult, I still have to remind myself that no one said life was going to be fair. My kids' school closed because of low enrollment—not fair. I missed a writing opportunity—not fair. A scheduling conflict means I couldn't get to a program I'd wanted to attend—not fair. In these moments, I have to look at what I think I'm missing out on. What is it that I thought I had some kind of right to? Is there another plan, maybe one I can't see yet? Can I trust that God's got this?

Ultimately, fairness isn't what we need. Love is what we need. Often that means taking action, making things happen, and serving others. In losing Ethan, I learned that love also means letting myself be cared for. I don't get to choose where, when, or in what circumstances I'm going to need that care. Accepting the crosses I'm given means surrendering to God's will. It means accepting that my plans just aren't going to happen, that life is going to look different than I thought it would.

If I am living for myself, this is a hurdle to overcome. But if I am living for God and for his kingdom, this is a way to draw closer to him, an obstacle to endure together with my Lord, a painful but fruitful opportunity to place my whole self in my Father's loving and capable hands.

• • • • • • • • • • • • • • • • • • • •

REFLECT

- What major and minor crosses did you carry before you became a parent? How have they affected your parenting, for better or for worse?
- What crosses are you carrying now, in your present stage of parenthood? How has your faith and the Church helped you to bear them?
- To what other kinds of crosses do you compare your own? What comes of this line of thinking? How can you better use this reflection to build up the kingdom of God?

• • • • • • • • • • • • • • • • • • • •

PRAY

Lord Jesus, you promise that your burden is easy and your yoke is light (see Matthew 11:30). Help me to accept the challenges

I'll face today with courage, grace, and trust in your Father's will for me.

•••••••••••••••••••

CALL ON THE COMMUNION OF SAINTS

The Catholic Church does not have an official teaching on what happens to miscarried children after death. However, even though they were not baptized, these children also never had the capacity to sin. Because of our Lord's great mercy, we can hope and pray that they rest in their Father's arms, where they can intercede for those of us still in this world.

Sweet Ethan, and all babies lost before birth, pray for us.

FOUR

ON THE POWER OF PRAYER

IT'S GOING TO BE OKAY

My kids are little enough yet that when something goes wrong, they usually come to me to have it fixed. A toy breaks, and I get out the superglue. Someone falls down, and I kiss where it hurts. A coughing fit keeps someone up at night, and I hook up the nebulizer. "It's okay," I tell them. "It's going to be fine." They trust that as their mother, I can make things better. I love when I can. As they get older, I know there are going to be more and more times when I can't.

Sometimes, even now, the best I can do for my children is hold them close and offer up a prayer. Those pleas can be desperate and sometimes get offered up as a last-ditch effort rather than as the first order of business. I do my best to make it right and then beg the Lord to step in when I feel helpless or hopeless. I can't help but think, *If I'm the mother, aren't I supposed to be able to make this better?* Time and again, God answers me: "Can I help?"

• • • • • • • • • • • • • • • • • • • •

We told basically everyone we knew about baby number two within a week of getting a positive pregnancy test. I don't buy into the wait-until-the-end-of-the-first-trimester thing. Just weeks prior, I'd told John that should we ever suffer a miscarriage, I'd want everyone to know so they could pray for us and so it wouldn't be awkward to have to say, "Well, I was pregnant, but now I'm not."

Maybe it made it a little easier to share the news, but it still wasn't actually easy. I found the announcement we'd sent to our friends via email, hit "reply all," and bluntly stated that our child didn't have a heartbeat at the twelve-week ultrasound. We asked for their prayers as we grieved and tried to find peace.

In the weeks and months that followed, I had trouble sleeping at night, in part because I didn't know where to put my hands. I'm a side sleeper and had gotten used to resting my hands on my belly, near my baby, while I fell asleep. Now, that felt wrong. There was no one in there to connect with. I didn't want to touch the emptiness. It took me a long time to remember that I used to sleep with my hands under my pillow. When I did, I couldn't understand why it had taken me so long to recall what used to be a natural, unconscious position.

In that time, I experienced such grief that I couldn't pray. I didn't have trouble getting into a still, quiet place, but then I didn't know what to do. I didn't know what to say. John and I had a routine of saying a Rosary together in the evenings after Jacob was in bed. But now I couldn't speak my portions of the prayers out loud for crying. Some nights I couldn't even make it through grace at dinner without choking on tears. Prayer brought me to the reality of the situation: I would never hold this child I loved so dearly in my arms. Before I could meet him face-to-face, he was already gone. He was a blank. I was a blank.

I could not pray, but other people could. And they did. My parents called me every day, just to say hi and see how I was doing. My brothers-in-law on the other side of the country, one of them still in college at the time, handwrote us letters affirming our family, our faith, and their love for us. One of my best friends since kindergarten visited one afternoon, insisting that I take a nap while she played with Jacob. Another came to Brooklyn from Boston for all of twenty-four hours, just to be with me for a little while. Masses were said for us and for Ethan. His name was inscribed in the Book of Life at the Church of the Holy Innocents in Manhattan, where every month Mass would be offered for him and others who died before birth.

These are all prayers, even those that didn't take place in a church or in silence. In a variety of ways, these are the means by which the people who care about us offered something up for us. Their sacrifices became graces in my life. There were times when I thought I could actually feel hands holding me up and guiding me through caring for Jacob, even though I didn't want to get out of bed in the morning. I was angry, and I didn't understand why this had happened. When I thought about it, I was almost surprised that I didn't feel myself drifting away from my faith. Instead, I felt myself pulled in closer. I felt drawn into my Father's embrace. I was broken, but I was loved. Things would, somehow, someday, be okay.

When I was young, my mom told me that God answers every prayer, but he doesn't always say yes. I wasn't going to get my baby back, but I could allow myself to rest in my Father's arms.

I could rage and push away, or I could settle in, close my eyes, and take a deep breath. I could choose to hear his voice telling me, "Come here. I will hold you. It will be okay."

Because I had nothing to say, I was more able to listen. I recalled the words I'd heard deep inside when I first got the news, the message that this wasn't my fault. That moment continued to give me a strong sense of peace, and even more so when I came to understand it as the voice of my Ethan, who was already gone, who was already at the feet of Jesus, interceding for me, for our family, and for his brother and the siblings still to come. I learned to ask for his help when I feel scared, lost, or helpless. I trust him. I know I want to be where he is, and that helps remind me that prayer should be my first recourse.

After hearing another mother's story about how the children she'd lost to miscarriage helped her and her husband find a lost set of car keys, I also started to ask Ethan to help me find things. I figure St. Anthony of Padua is borderline overworked, as is St. Boniface, especially by the English-speaking population.

One evening I was looking for something in my bedroom. I thought it was in a particular bag, but I couldn't find it. I asked Ethan. I received a sense of peace and the understanding that I should go to bed. When I woke the next morning, I had an urge to return to that same bag. In the next moment, I had what I'd been looking for. The thing itself wasn't as important as the reminder that I am not alone in trying to live my life for the Lord. There are helps in place for me. I only need to call on them.

I'd had a couple of experiences like this before John lost his wedding ring in the Atlantic Ocean. One of our children elected to hold John's ring rather than his finger when jumping over a wave. A combination of sunscreen, sand, and water made the ring slip, and off it went, into the sea. I was taking Sarah for a walk while all this happened and had trouble believing the news when I met John and the boys back on the beach.

John and I had been married almost seven years. I knew losing the ring didn't make the sacrament any less valid, but still. The ring was a sign of that covenant. It was engraved with a message from me to John. It was blessed on the same day we promised ourselves to each other until death did us part. The sentimental value was profound.

Immediately, I asked Ethan to help.

We told the nearby lifeguard, who didn't offer much in the way of hope. When we came back the next day, he told us some beachcombers with metal detectors had found a few rings the evening before, but the lifeguard didn't know which was ours. It felt like a tragically lost opportunity, and I was helpless to right it. I prayed again.

John and I tried to play with the kids, but we couldn't help incessantly scanning the sand and the waves, jumping at anything that glinted in the sun. We were due to leave the shore the next day. We briefly considered coming back to the beach that evening when the folks with metal detectors would be out again. But the hour the lifeguard suggested was the kids' bedtime. We needed to pack. It was crazy to think we'd ever see the ring again. Still, I kept praying.

I was so sad. The whole thing didn't feel real. Wedding rings are supposed to stay put! But things don't always do what they're supposed to. I knew things could be worse, but I still couldn't get my mind off the ring.

What the lifeguard had said about people routinely searching the beach with metal detectors stuck with me. I went online that evening and discovered the Lost and Found page on Craigslist. I posted the time and place we'd lost the ring, what it looked like, and the carefully chosen message engraved inside. I felt silly when I told John what I'd done. He is more logical and rational than I am, and I thought maybe I was being unreasonable to not let go and move on. But I had to try.

The next day, I received an email from a man who offered to look for the ring for us for a small fee. John called him back, and he gave us some advice about the listing. He said we should add "Reward if found" but also warned us that people sometimes read pages like these to find things to search for and then sell elsewhere. Now we knew that even if someone found it, they weren't necessarily going to give it back. We'd hopped up another peg on the hopeless scale, and I'd just about given up.

I didn't understand why John wasn't at the jeweler's shop the next day, ordering a new ring. He was waiting, he told me, for the coupon the jeweler sent us every year on our anniversary, which was only six weeks away. A much calmer individual than I in situations like this, John could wait.

A week later, we were out for a fancy birthday dinner date. When John left the table for a moment, I took out my phone and checked my email.

Someone had found our ring.

It felt impossible, but I knew it wasn't.

It seemed that this young man had found the ring on the beach that first night. A fellow ring hunter saw the Craigslist ad a few days later and told him about it the next time she saw him.

All the pieces that had made us feel as if the ring was farther and farther from us turned out to be part of the plan to bring it back to us. I was awestruck, humbled. It's much easier to say I trust in God and his plan than to actually do it. And yet here I was seeing things fit together, like a glimpse into the bigger plan for our lives. Through prayer, I could see how one little ring made its way out of the Atlantic Ocean and back onto John's finger. It was as if God were saying, "See? I told you it would be okay."

Having faith means believing that every kind of brokenness will eventually be made whole. All that is lost will be found. All that is in darkness will come to light.

The saga of the ring reaffirmed for us that people aren't always greedy. Things aren't always what you'd expect. Still, I know that not every loss is going to be reconciled in my lifetime. I know I can't see all of God's plan. Really, I can't see most of it, like how icebergs are 95 percent under water. But when I'm able, through God's grace, to really trust that things are going to be okay, life as a whole is easier to take. When I recognize how much is beyond my control, I spend less time trying to resist God's call and more time rejoicing in it. When things aren't up to me, I see more clearly that everything is a gift.

Getting married and putting that ring on John's finger was a tremendous blessing, the greatest of my life. Losing it was painful. Getting it back was a miracle. The problem was truly too big for us to handle on our own. We couldn't comb the whole ocean. The waves are always moving; there are people and creatures in and out of it all the time; it stretches halfway around the world. But for some reason, God decided it would be good for the ring to make its way back to us. In that, we saw the power of our child's prayer for us. The symbol of our insoluble union went through a lot but came back intact, still whole, ready to get back to work.

•••••••••••••••••••

REFLECT

- When have you given a seemingly impossible situation up to God? What helped you do it? What was the result?
- How do you react when something painful happens? Is your first instinct prayer? What do you pray?
- When you panic over a situation, what feelings lie at the root of that reaction?

• • • • • • • • • • • • • • • • • • •

PRAY

Lord, when I lose something—be it an item, an important paper, my keys, or my cool—help me to turn to you first. You are the giver of all that is good. Help me to trust in you.

• • • • • • • • • • • • • • • • • • •

CALL ON THE COMMUNION OF SAINTS

St. Anthony of Padua, a Franciscan friar, is the patron of lost things. He had an excellent memory and such a tremendous knowledge of the faith that he was proclaimed a Doctor of the Church. Whether we have lost our phones, a child's other shoe, or more significantly, our faith, hope, and trust in the Lord, St. Anthony's intercession can help us retrieve it.

St. Anthony of Padua, pray for us!

FIVE

ON CARING FOR OUR BODIES

EAT YOUR DINNER

As much as I care about the nutrition my children get, I can relate to their whims. Chicken fingers and fish sticks are delicious. I could eat garlic bread for days. The kids get their collective sweet tooth largely from me, so to contain it, we have a regular schedule for dessert nights: weekends and Tuesdays, as well as birthdays, baptismal days, and feast days. This is not enough for my dear Henry, who for a while was in the habit of asking me if we could have dessert on other nights "just for fun."

"Dessert is always just for fun," I told him. "Good try, though."

For most of my life, I compartmentalized my physical well-being and my spiritual well-being. I knew I had both a body and a soul and that they were somehow linked to who I was. I was grateful I'd never broken a bone or had a serious illness, but that was all the connection I was capable of seeing between the two.

The reality is that my body is more than the sensory headquarters of my being. It is a temple of the Holy Spirit, a gift from God to be used to love him and to share that love with others (see 1 Corinthians 6:19). I can choose either to take care of that gift, to honor it and use it for God's glory, or to neglect it and let the (potato) chips fall where they may, probably into the folds of the couch.

Like so many women, I've long struggled with body issues. I was never the skinniest kid in school, and there was an awkward chunky phase around fifth grade, right about the time I got glasses and started orthodontia. In high school, I managed to play four years of field hockey, but I was by far the slowest runner on our losing team. I got good grades easily enough. I accepted that my strength was in my brain and the rest would just have to do.

After I had my first child, I started to see my body in a different light. It had carried this little guy from conception to birth and then sustained him for another six months before we introduced any other food. When I got down on myself about something that didn't fit or about not liking what I saw in pictures of myself, I reminded myself what my body was capable of, what a gift it was to literally grow our family. I was starting to connect the spiritual and physical aspects of my being. I was grateful. Mostly.

Nine months after Sarah was born, my body still looked more postpartum than I thought it should. It felt that way too. I was often cranky and tired and not exactly motivated to get involved with what the kids were doing. I found a scale to step on and did the math. I was overweight and less than a year from turning thirty. I knew that getting into better shape was only going to get harder as I got older. If I wanted to make a change, I needed to start now. I realized how much time I was spending worrying about how I looked, the clothes I would wear, and what I would eat.

Wait a minute. Isn't there a line in scripture about that? "Do not worry about your life, what you will eat (or drink); or about your body, what you will wear. Is not life more than food and the body more than clothing?" (Mt 6:25).

Of course life is more than these things. My worries were a waste of time, but they came so naturally. How I'd rather use that time to laugh with my kids, to encourage them to grow into themselves, and to give them an example of a woman pleased and grateful for the way God made her. I am the woman my children—boys and girl alike—see most often. Like it or not, my behavior will have an impact on what they learn to see as normal.

I wasn't practicing what I was preaching to my kids about eating well. It occurred to me that my crankiness might be beyond par for the course of the mother of little ones. There might be a way I could fix it, at least in part, if I started taking better care of the body I was gifted.

With young kids, finding an hour to hit the gym or even twenty minutes to prepare healthy meals and snacks felt like a luxury. But the alternative was putting the wrong stuff in my system and then struggling through increasingly stressful days without the required sustenance. This felt anything but luxurious. I was accustomed to praying for the faith, hope, and love I needed to get through the day. I needed to start eating in a way that nourished me and allowed my body to do what it was meant to do—to let the things I consumed be an active prayer of thanksgiving for my physical form.

With the help of a friend for accountability, I made a decision to put myself a little earlier in the priority lineup—not to indulge myself but to take care of myself. I changed what I ate, when I ate, and how long I slept, and I tallied how much water I drank in a day. I added in supplements and started to notice how great my body felt when I fed it what it needed. I remember thinking to myself, *This is the way I was made to feel.*

My lifestyle tweaks weren't reserved for my plate and my sleep schedule. I carved out time for reading in the morning and at night. When I woke up, I stretched for a few minutes and worked my way up to an almost three-minute plank. I took time for focused just-me-and-God prayer time, which had largely fallen by the wayside. Every day I felt more energized. I started to make better choices. I continued to eat better. I enjoyed exercising more, so I did it more. I was moving more and sitting less. I lost some weight, but what was more important was that I lost that nagging part of me that kept saying I wasn't enough. I felt taken care of, and I wanted to do that more for others. These things took only a few minutes a day, and yet they left me with so much more time and mental space to devote to where God was calling me.

Soon, I wasn't worried about being too big for my clothes; they were too big for me. The tables had turned, and now I *had* to go shopping (yay!). I took the opportunity to make thoughtful decisions about who I was as a mother and as a daughter of God. I chose styles that made me feel I'd gotten dressed on purpose but remained functional for the thousand times I wash my hands each day and the frequent trips to the floor to clean something up or to be a horsey to the rhythm of the William Tell Overture for my little girl.

Attention from others is obviously not the goal, but people noticed. When I changed what I was putting in, I changed what I was giving out. I was more patient with the kids and happier in my own skin. I was wowed yet again at what God had created in my body: new life, or maybe renewed life. We all know, in theory, what it takes to care for ourselves. When I made an effort to put all that into action, I found that—surprise, surprise—God cares just as much about what I eat as I care about what my kids eat. Our health is sometimes beyond our control. But not all the time.

It feels good to feel strong, capable, and ready to serve. Caring for my kids is still a largely physical endeavor, but the state of my brain matters too. I need to be "on" to have a good conversation with my kindergartener after school. I can't be cranky at lunchtime because I didn't eat a good breakfast and now feel lethargic. My bedtime is directly related to my capacity for patience the following day. It's not fair for my kids to have to deal with the repercussions of my desire to stay up late watching one more episode of *The Crown*.

Neither a good diet nor regular physical activity needs to cost much of anything. You know what's a good on-the-go snack? An apple. A banana. A pear. Carrot sticks. A gym membership may be great motivation for some, but there are benefits to a simpler regimen too—a vigorous walk with a friend, or if you're feeling a little more twenty-first century, a free online workout video. Really, it's all the other stuff—the makeup, the fads, the disposable clothing, and the quick fixes—that are the add-ons. When I got back to basics, when I took honest care of the body I was given, I found how little of all the rest of it I needed. I learned that I don't need more than who I was made to be.

Our culture constantly tells us women in particular that physically we are not good enough. Marketers have all sorts of solutions, from lotions to food and clothing to procedures. I know this is a load of lies, but the tricky thing is that I interpreted the wrong message when I read more encouraging blogs or women's magazines instead. These told me that I am perfect just the way I am because I am made in God's image and likeness. Fact. But I inferred from that that trying, or even wanting, to change anything about myself was wrong. This is fiction.

I am called to love the body I live in. Love is action, so that means making sure there are enough leafy greens and brightly colored fruits on my plate to sustain the gift of my body. A healthy lifestyle is not a luxury; it's a responsibility to God, to my family, to my community, and to myself.

When my son was given a set of football-player figurines for Christmas, he instantly turned the goalposts into weapons, like Teenage Mutant Ninja Turtle Raphael's twin sai. I told him to be careful; this was a gift, and he should use it as it was intended, so that he didn't break it.

As a daughter of God, I have the same responsibility. My body is a gift. It is how I receive the Body and Blood of Christ each day. It is what allows me to put my vocation into action and serve our Lord in kisses and snuggles, in games of hide and seek, in building sand castles at the beach, and in taking walks on cool autumn days. My Father cares about what I put into my body, just as he cares about what I choose to produce out of it.

• • • • • • • • • • • • • • • • • • •

REFLECT

- How does the way you treat your body honor God? What area of wellness could you focus more on to live better and serve God more fully?

- What example are you setting for your children with the way you care for yourself? Are you practicing what you preach to them?
- What stands between you and more healthful living? Is it worth it?

• • • • • • • • • • • • • • • • • • • •

PRAY

Lord, Creator of heaven and earth and Creator of this body of mine, guide me to good lifestyle choices today, in what I eat and drink, in how I choose to be active, and when I take a much-needed rest. Help me to consider the consequences of how I care for myself, so that I am ready to serve you as your hands and feet.

• • • • • • • • • • • • • • • • • • • •

CALL ON THE COMMUNION OF SAINTS

St. John Paul II is well known for the series of Wednesday audiences he gave between 1979 and 1984, illuminating the connection between our physical beings and our souls. Now known as the Theology of the Body, his teachings reveal the true nature of sexuality, as well as an appreciation for the bodies that we live our earthly lives in. They are a gift to be handled with care.

St. John Paul II, pray for us.

SIX

ON THE IMPORTANCE OF REST

GO TO BED

How is it that each of my children came to learn the timeworn tricks of asking for water, the bathroom, another story, another kiss, or a third hug after the lights have been turned out? I certainly didn't teach them these things. The oldest doesn't even have an older cousin to show him the nocturnal ropes of childhood. It must be instinct.

As incredulous as I can be that my super-tired children want to stay up later, I am no better at protecting my own shut-eye. There's always something else to do that seems like a good idea until I'm peeling myself out of bed the next morning. I know lack of sleep, like poor nutrition, makes me cranky and impatient. Sleep deprivation takes such a toll on me that sometimes I wonder why God made me a mother. A more experienced mom once told me, "Each time you have a child, you commit to not sleeping for five years." I've yet to disprove this theory.

I know I'm not the only one in this situation. Not getting enough rest is one of the things we moms tend to humblebrag about. "Mine was up twice last night." "Mine was up every hour." "Mine wouldn't let me put him down, and when I did, his sister woke up." We run on fumes and accept it as the norm. To a certain extent, this is reality for those with young children, but as with my nutrition, there is some responsibility I need to take as well.

If I look closely at my intentions, I can see that in the moments I choose something over rest, my decisions are more about escaping from realities that feel overwhelming than feeding a part of my mind or my soul. I easily fall into the trap of trying to accomplish more and more just so I can tell myself I did something objectively worthwhile. Evening hours vanish as if they were seconds. My perspective is focused on how I think the rest of the world sees me and what will make me feel I have earned my keep as a person taking up space on this planet today. I'm trying to fill a hole left open by my lack of trust in God's love for me, although I know I won't fill it with anything except prayer and his grace.

Physical rest is important, but the spiritual component of the changes I made had further-reaching effects for me. My typical smattering of prayer throughout the day when I was about to lose my cool or when I heard someone was sick wasn't enough. "Be still," the Lord tells me, "and know that I am God" (Ps 46:11). This is a truth I can settle into, a place where I can relax and let my soul recharge. Adding this time to the beginning and end of my day changed everything in between.

When I stopped trying to feel whole on my own and let God back into the picture on a personal level, my priorities shifted. With consistent prayer, even for a short time each day, I started to find enough time to get my house and professional work done. My vision shifted from this world into the next. I became more discerning about completing tasks that actually matter and letting the chaff fall away. I remembered to be concerned with what God thinks of the way I'm spending the time he's gifted me. I reflected on whether I was using my strengths and the challenges presented to me to serve him, to grow closer to him, to depend on him, and to love. It made making decisions about how to spend my time simpler. I realized that if I never slow down, I'll burn out and I won't be able to serve. I need that stillness to reboot.

One Saturday morning in the middle of Jacob's first year in school full time—with karate and piano lessons to boot—our pastor gave a homily about truly respecting the Sabbath. He impressed on us the need to not do grocery shopping or conduct any sort of business—not clean, not do any work—but truly rest as God did on the last day. I'd heard this message before, but it seemed impossible. Taking it a little bit easier had seemed all we could manage. But perhaps because I'd already started to make the connection between my body and soul and how their well-being relates to my vocation, my heart was ready for more—or less—now. I saw that I needed this day of rest. God had created me to need this day of rest! John and I discussed it right after Mass and decided it was time that we made this commandment a more serious priority.

The first weekend was tough. I hadn't prepared for it and thus needed to do two days' work in one. Before I got too frustrated, I looked at my calendar and tried to figure out what I needed to do to make the next Sunday more restful. I'd have to do laundry on a schedule. I'd have to meal-plan on Friday so I could shop on Saturday. There were things we'd have to say no to.

By holding each other accountable, John and I have been able to stick with resting on the Sabbath. Suddenly, we had time to play music together as a family. Jacob's piano lessons bore fruit for all of us. While he played the keyboard, John returned to the violin that had been waiting patiently in the basement for us to get our act together. I started to knit more and finally made the socks I'd been promising Jacob for months.

I began to enjoy our family more. I felt, on these Sundays in particular, that I was really seeing my kids. We weren't rushing anywhere. We weren't too busy to make use of the toys and books we had all over the house. I couldn't pull a "I want to play with you too, but first I have to . . ." because there was nothing else to do.

Resting on Sunday—no major chores, no professional work at all—sets the tone for the week, but it's not enough for me. I'm learning that in order to function best, my body needs a good chunk of sleep at night and my mind needs quiet time for at least twenty minutes midday. Like healthy meals, this might seem luxurious. Rest remains discouragingly undervalued in our culture's go-go-go mentality. Even to me, it still seems that maybe I'm slacking off when I choose to let myself sit down.

But with little kids, I am talking, moving, and being touched almost all the time. I can't do it for twelve hours straight. My inner introvert needs a little while to be alone and quiet. I have a limit, and when it's reached, I need the humility to power down and recharge.

God is not surprised by this. Of his ten commandments, "Keep holy the Sabbath" ranks at number three. He knows that to be who he made me to be, I need to step away from the things of the world now and then and spend time with my Lord. Every day I need to remember why I'm here, what I'm working to build, and to whom it is that I belong. On Sunday, it's not enough to go to Mass, maybe have a nicer breakfast than normal, and then go do all the stuff I didn't manage to do the previous week. The Sabbath is a full day, one-seventh of my entire life. I don't deserve my time on earth; I haven't earned it. Every moment is a gift and should be rightly treated as such.

Life is complicated and messy. With kids, it is also unpredictable. But I'd argue there actually is enough time to get it all done. I just have to be careful about what I perceive as "all." Is it what I think the world expects of me? Or is it what God needs from me?

As I write this, I am preparing for my first marathon. In reading through the training program, I found this: "Scientists suggest that it is during the rest period (the twenty-four to seventy-two hours between hard bouts of exercise) that the muscles actually regenerate and get stronger. Coaches also will tell you that you can't run hard unless you are well rested. And it is hard running (such as the long run) that allows you to improve."[5] In the spiritual realm as well, it is rest that provides the strength I need to persevere in the next big push.

I am not a robot. I am not the Energizer Bunny. I cannot keep going and going and going. I will crash. I've been there, and it's not a good time for anyone. Resting with purpose, rather than because I've collapsed from exhaustion, makes me feel like a brand-new person. Not feeling overwhelmed and lost can take some getting used to, but it's much better than the alternative.

When everything stops, I can catch back up to myself. I can hear myself think and register what has happened so far in the day and refocus on where God is leading me next. Naps aren't just for babies. Quiet time doesn't mean you're in trouble. Detoxing from the more trying elements of the day is just another means of refueling. I have lived the proof that taking breaks is key to my serving fully in my vocation.

It's happened more than once that I'm on a roll with well-timed and productive rests, and then something keeps me up too late again. In a single day, I see things go back to how they used to be. There is only one variable in this experiment, and the conclusion is clear. When I don't take that break, I get all wrapped up in myself and lose my direction. I listen to the world around me. I listen to myself complain. When I fix the problem at its root, I hear God again and I am able to recognize and respond to his call.

Now when someone pretend-complains about lack of sleep, I fight the urge to play along. Instead, I try to go to bed a little earlier that night, so I can serve well the next day. When I respect the rhythms of life—of a day, a season, or a year—I stay closer to who God wants me to be.

• • • • • • • • • • • • • • • • • • •

REFLECT

- What kind of rest do you need to be your best self? What is keeping you from getting it?
- If circumstances are beyond your control, how can you choose to offer the sacrifice up to God more willingly?
- Do your husband and kids know what rest looks like to you? Have you told them what you need, so they can help you achieve it? You are not an island!

• • • • • • • • • • • • • • • • • •

PRAY

Lord, thank you for giving me a body and mind that are capable of so much. Please help me to care for them well so that I know what it is to rest in your arms. Help me to be conscious of your presence when things get busy—or better, before!

• • • • • • • • • • • • • • • • • •

CALL ON THE COMMUNION OF SAINTS

More than once, St. Peter, an apostle and the first pope, experienced firsthand the saving power of calling on the Lord. Time and again he also witnessed Jesus taking time to rest in the arms of his Father. Through Jesus' own example, Peter learned the demands of following the Lord as well as the necessity of rest to recharge ourselves and ultimately serve more fully.

St. Peter, pray for us.

SEVEN

ON PATIENCE AS A NECESSARY VIRTUE

WAIT A MINUTE

When you don't yet have a concept of time, the phrase "Wait a minute" is meaningless. Ask my daughter, who spends weekdays in the car with me driving back and forth to my sons' school. I try to anticipate what she'll want in the car or what I think she'll need—snack cup with pretzels, snack cup with cereal, water, stuffed cow, stuffed dinosaur, or stuffed superhero bunny—but it feels as if I get it wrong all the time. Telling her she can have whatever it is when we get home, in X minutes, or just "soon" might alleviate her anxiety for a few minutes, but it rarely lasts for long. "Soon" doesn't mean much when you're not yet two years old.

Even if she could wrap her head around the concept, she doesn't want animal crackers soon; she wants them now. All she can see is this moment, when Mommy isn't giving her what she's asking for. And that, of course, makes her angry.

For those of us who are supposed to be mature enough to understand the passage of time and how different circumstances can make it seem swift or slow, being patient can still be a challenge. Humans have a tendency to be self-serving, and our culture celebrates and encourages instant gratification in children as much as adults.

Patience is far from my strongest virtue, so I often pray to grow in it. Silly me. I'd hoped my asking would make me magically more patient, preferably overnight or sooner. But the good stuff requires something of a struggle. Be careful what you wish for? I'd say be careful what you pray for—you might just get an opportunity to make it happen.

Young children are little mirrors of their parents' attitudes, behaviors, and language. It's funny when your kid starts to use an adult phrase, such as "in the nick of time," and you can tell he got it from you. Big words in small mouths are adorable. Adult behavior, especially the things we're not quite so proud of, can have a more humbling effect when we see it in our kids.

For the first two years of my parenting, I wasn't a yeller. I didn't have much reason to be. I had one little boy who I knew wasn't capable of rationalizing whether or not it was wise to dump his Cheerios out. He only knew it would make a good sound and it was more fun to eat directly off the table. As his decision-making process became more complex and we added more little hands to dump more exciting things on the kitchen table (and elsewhere), the volume of my voice likewise increased. For a while it was a steady increase throughout the day or over the course of a few days. Finally, my frustrations reached a point that I just figured the kids were going to do something to set me off, intentional or not, and I jumped right to yelling.

It wasn't until I heard my older son yell at my younger son that I realized how terrible this sounded. There was no doubt he'd learned this reaction to things not going his way from me. I could tell from the tone and the phrasing he used. *Oh my goodness*, I thought. *I did this. I have to fix it. But how?*

I knew it was going to take longer to change this behavior than it did to instill it, so I had my work cut out for me. Intellectually, I believed that some circumstances required yelling—a child running into a busy parking lot, for example—but most others did not. That's not how I was parenting, though, and it's not how my children were learning to deal with situations that upset them.

I slowed down and listened more to the language I was using when I started to yell. I discovered that most of the times when I got ramped up, my reaction was based in selfish thoughts. I was exhausted, I was interrupted in trying to get something done, or I just didn't want to have so much noise in the house for a little while. Me, me, me. I wasn't in control, and I didn't like it.

In the many times I brought this to Confession, I was often told to be sure I was taking care of myself, that I was making whatever recharged me a priority. (There's that rest again!) I am only human, and I certainly have limits. Ignoring them was setting us all up to fail.

Kids have limits too. I had been forgetting that my kids are, in fact, children. Sometimes they act out of line, but most of the time, they're just being their developmentally appropriate selves. I wasn't giving them room to do that.

Little brothers and sisters are prone to mess up things their older siblings have created. The way clumsier hands play often means the tumble of a delicately engineered tower or a tear in a just-completed coloring page. "She's little," we tell the older child. "Be patient. She didn't mean it; she's still learning."

When I started to listen to what I was saying as if God were saying it to me, I realized that I'm still learning too. To grow in patience—with my children, God, and myself—is another way of saying, "Trust in the Lord." He has a plan. I shouldn't need any proof of this, and yet he's proven to me time and again that he knows best, he knows more. He knows me better than I know myself, and he loves me for exactly who I am.

The catch, if you will, is that God can't really put his plan into action until I give him my *fiat*, my yes. Our Blessed Mother Mary is the ultimate disciple because she gave that to God, fully and joyfully, her whole life in perfect surrender. It was never about her, so there was nothing to make her impatient. She held things in her heart, but she didn't cling to them for dear life. Her life was lived for something, somewhere, and someone else. If I aspire to do the same, it means living on God's time, surrendering my plans, and letting go of the facade of control.

When my sister-in-law shared Henri Nouwen's *Spirituality of Waiting* with me after we lost Ethan, I was struck by his suggestion that waiting—being patient—is an active response to a situation. "A patient person is a person who dares to stay where she is," Nouwen says, "who dares to taste the moment to the full. If anything is happening, it's happening here and now. . . . If it's not happening now, it's not happening ever!"[6] God is right here, right now, in this moment, even if it's not the moment in which I expect to see God.

Am I about to blow my top with three kids asking me for different things at the same time? This is an opportunity to grow in patience. Am I worried about sending my kid with food allergies on that field trip? This is an opportunity to grow in trust (and check the expiration date on his EpiPen). Do I feel I can't go on another moment without taking a break to have a few minutes of impossible silence? This is an opportunity to make a sacrifice, to put someone else before myself, even though I've already been doing that all day.

The deeper I get into this journey of motherhood, into my vocation to serve the Lord, the more I understand that it is when I am weak that I am strong (see 2 Corinthians 12:10). My strength lies not in my magically learning more parenting skills but in direct correspondence with the Lord during peaceful, uninterrupted prayer time. It's not about giving me a greater capacity to do anything, unless that thing is leaning on the Lord—resting in him, trusting in him, and letting a whole lot of stuff go.

Just as Christ did on the Cross, it means surrender.

Nouwen also considers, "We have come to live in a way that we always think that the real thing is happening tomorrow. . . . We don't fully taste what's happening."[7] How often have I said something like, "I can't wait until he can crawl," "I can't wait until she pops that tooth," "Well, when he's in school, it will be different," and so on? God gave me this moment, now. Here. Today. There's nothing wrong with looking forward to something I expect in the future, but it can't be at the detriment of the present. Every moment is an opportunity to love the Lord. Some are more challenging than others. But any one I try to gloss over, to skip to get on to the next thing, is a missed opportunity to receive God's grace.

There will come a time when our house is quiet. I don't want it to be because I shushed my kids so much as little children that they learned I'm not interested in what's important to them. I want it to be because they saw in me an example of how to lean on Christ and they are out in the world, serving him as his hands and feet, however they are called. My vocation is to guide them to theirs. Even though I am not a religious sister as St. Thérèse of

Lisieux was, I believe her words apply to me too: "My vocation is to love."

I want to build relationships now that last into the teenage years and straight through to adulthood. God wants the same in his relationship with me. I want to enjoy and cherish the time I have with my kids when they are young and irrational and mostly concerned with what household objects they can reimagine as laser blasters. And really, that's just about everything.

Not to get too hokey, but we really don't know what kind of time we have with each other. We are bound to live in the moment. This is where God is. I can see him in the little faces that have my husband's eyes and my teeth, my husband's dark hair or my lighter eyes. Yet what's most imperative that I see in their faces is not a reflection of my husband or me but the image of God.

I need to see that image of God when I look in the mirror too. If I let him, God will work in my life. If I ask, he will offer me his mercy. But he's not necessarily going to do it on my time. There are times when he is going to ask me to wait. It doesn't mean he's going away. Rather, it means that he wants me to draw closer to him, so that I can conform my will to his.

I still yell at my children more than I should. I haven't mastered patience and self-surrender, but I know it's the path I want to be on. I am more aware of the impact my impatience has on my children, our family as a whole, and my own soul. I can see that the change must begin with me. When I yell less, the kids speak more kindly to each other. When I leave room for kids to be kids, we all have more fun together. When I realize I've lost my temper, I try to take a moment to calm down. I acknowledge that I've made a mistake, and I ask forgiveness, which my children, especially the older ones, are always willing to give. I'm not perfect, but I can strive for peacefulness.

Sometimes, in the car, my daughter asks for exactly what I know she needs. I pass back the cup and am gifted a delighted smile with a triumphant giggle that melts my heart. I am satisfied to know I have offered her something that will feed her, if only on a physical level.

How much more joyful is the Lord, when he gives me what I need and I accept it with a grateful heart?

• • • • • • • • • • • • • • • • • •

REFLECT

- In what situations do you find yourself impatient? What's the deeper cause?
- Ask the Holy Spirit to guide you toward a virtue in which you can grow. How does a lack of trust factor into your weakness?
- How valuable is control to you in your marriage, your family life, or your daily schedule? What might happen if you let some of that go?

• • • • • • • • • • • • • • • • • •

PRAY

Lord, I trust that you have a plan for my life and for my family. Help me to trust in that plan and surrender to it, so that you might use me to bring more souls to heaven.

• • • • • • • • • • • • • • • • • • • •

CALL ON THE COMMUNION OF SAINTS

We know from stories of her life that St. Thérèse of Lisieux was an extremely emotional child. Yet when she fully accepted the Lord into her heart, her outbursts ceased. She was so humble, so in love with the Lord, that what she wanted didn't matter to her anymore. She made hundreds of small but powerful sacrifices to conform her will to the Lord's. It is this "little way" that elevated her not only to sainthood but also to be recognized as a Doctor of the Church.

St. Thérèse of Lisieux, pray for us.

EIGHT

ON LIVING COUNTERCULTURALLY

THAT'S NOT HOW WE BEHAVE IN THIS FAMILY

At six years old, Jacob had already complained about the minimal television we watch at home, relative to what his classmates purportedly viewed. Kindergarten showed him that in other houses, kids watch TV shows, movies, and—get this—the news more often than we do.

"Every family is different, buddy," I told him, "but God put you in this family, with these parents, and with these rules for a reason. We have to trust him." My explanation satisfied him in that moment, but I have no doubt the question will come up again. Unless I keep them in a bubble, my kids are going to come home with words and behaviors they learned from their friends, not all of which are going to reconcile with the set of values John and I are working to instill in them.

I took Jacob to Mass nearly every day when he was a baby. Even before he could speak, I tried to explain bits of the Mass to him, whispering the words of the priest into his ear at the consecration, carefully enunciating responses so that he'd learn them properly. I tried to show him, a little bit each time, why this was the most important thing we did every day. As he got older, he fidgeted, and I let him toddle around in the pew. But still, at the moment the priest elevated the Host, I drew his attention back to the altar.

"'Behold' means 'look,'" I'd say. "See? That's Jesus!" It occurred to me that he would have questions in the future, especially about those doctrines at odds with popular opinion. If it was my job to teach him the faith, then I'd better believe it myself. I needed to know what I stood for.

The older I get, the more experiences I have, and the more decisions I have to make about what I stand for, especially in order to lead my children to the truth, the more I am aware of the challenges of being countercultural. I went on a retreat in high school where we were encouraged to live our faith "out loud." Quietly professing belief wasn't enough; we were called to act on our convictions. Even as teenagers, we were called to do the right thing and make choices that would allow us to continue to follow Christ, despite any possibility—or probability—of conflicting with what it would seem everyone else was doing. If we wanted to be rebels, if we wanted to be truly countercultural, living as a Christian fit the bill. I think this was supposed to appeal to the edgier among us, but the phrasing stuck with me. Living a Christian life was going to be hard. It was going to be worth it.

In my first attempt at writing this chapter, I explored our journey with natural family planning, or NFP. The choice not to use contraception is certainly countercultural. And yet, if we'd chosen to use anything from birth control pills to condoms, there's a lot John and I would have missed out on in knowing ourselves, growing in our relationship, understanding my body in particular, and connecting our marriage to God's love for us.

NFP, also known as fertility-awareness-based methods, or FABMs, is a topic I write about often for *Verily*, an online women's magazine. Apart from the faith factor, I've done a good deal of research that shows FABMs are proven effective, are economical, are environmentally sound, and have no side effects. We've used FABMs for nearly ten years now, but ultimately the root of what draws me to them is deeper than any of those reasons. At the heart of the matter, I choose to abide by the house rules of the one holy, catholic, and apostolic Church.

I choose to trust that God called me to himself in the Church to guide me to him, to lead me in the path he intended for my life. There have been horrible abuses within the Church; of that, there is no doubt. There are also a lot of misunderstandings in mainstream media about what the Church teaches and, more importantly, why it teaches it. The traditions of the Church are never the work of a single person. The *Catechism of the Catholic Church* has an extensive historical basis, founded on the life's work of people dedicated and devoted to following the Lord. I trust there is wisdom in that which I do not yet and may not ever fully possess.

I might not like the rules all the time, and I may struggle to understand them, but I choose not to reject them. To the world, this can look like blind submission. It can look like a surrender of independence. In a way, of course, it is. But it is also a choice to defer to the Church Fathers in the same way that I hope my children will defer to me in matters concerning their physical and spiritual well-being.

When John and I tell the kids not to do something—jump on the couch, eat the food lodged in the back of the car seat, or practice karate in the house—we try, as often as we can, to explain why that choice is a poor one. In my experience with more profound decisions, there is always a reason for the Church's stance, but it's rarely at the surface. Often I need to start a few steps back in the process of logic to understand the "why."

For example, the media will report that the Catholic Church does not recognize gay marriage. I've yet to see a mainstream piece that explores what the Church professes marriage to be and why gay marriage doesn't fit into that understanding of the sacrament. We just hear, "Don't do that!" For a lot of us, that's not enough. So the Church goes deeper. Like a loving parent, it has a "why" and is happy to explain.

Our culture wants us to believe that we can pick and choose what is true for each of us, that we are each entitled to our own truth. It's unclear how deep that goes. Most of us can agree that murder is wrong, but we don't necessarily agree on the roots of those moral grounds. This sense of relativism, that each person is subject to the morality he or she chooses to be valid, is as silly as letting my children plan mealtime for the week. Sometimes they'll make good decisions, but too often they will base decisions on their whims, rather than on what is really good for them. They are too young to see the big picture and to fully understand the consequences of their actions. Twizzlers are fun but not for lunch three times a week.

Certainly adults are more mature, wiser, and more experienced. But I, for one, am still learning new things about my mind, body, and soul all the time. I appreciate having a centuries-old path that guides me toward my ultimate goal.

Being an adult doesn't mean I have it all figured out. Identifying myself as a Christian requires that profession. The reality is, we are all influenced by something. It may be our upbringings, what we read, the company we keep, the media, or the philosophies or theories we choose to make our own. We can be intentional about what we take in, or we can absorb whatever comes our way.

I've learned through exploring the whys of what I believe and practice as a Catholic that everything is connected—my thoughts, my words, and my actions. So it matters what I take in, what I spend my time doing. It matters how I use my body. It matters how I speak. These are all a reflection of the raw truth of what is at the center of my life.

There's a quote attributed to Fr. Pedro Arrupe, S.J., that counsels, "Nothing is more practical than finding God, that is, than falling in love in a quite absolute, final way. What you are in love with, what seizes your imagination, will affect everything. . . . Fall in love, stay in love, and it will decide everything."[8]

There are myriad voices vying for my attention, voices that, like them or not, are going to influence the way I live my life. What am I truly in love with? What am I allowing—or choosing—to form me? If I can't watch an episode of *Downton Abbey* without being compelled to speak with a British accent for the next twenty minutes, how can I believe that I can make a decision about something as significant as sex and not have it resonate in another part of my life? In this or any other decision that has tremendous consequences, I need to carefully consider where I will seek guidance.

Purity is often misunderstood as prudishness, but this virtue is about more than sex. It's about integrity, about having a goal and living toward it. If I'm not practicing it and striving toward it, my kids aren't going to learn it. They won't have a way to know what it looks like. It seems like a tall order, but I have to remember that I'm not in this alone. God never intended me to raise my kids on my own, without his help. He doesn't expect me to live a life of purity without his guidance and graces.

When I claim God as my Father, I agree to live in his house, by his rules. It won't always seem fair. It's definitely not going to be what other people are doing. But this is the family I choose to be part of. I have been called as a daughter of God, and I want every aspect of my life to respond with a big, out-loud *yes*.

· · · · · · · · · · · · · · · · · · ·

REFLECT

- What aspect of your faith is challenging for you to live right now? How can you make a stronger effort to understand why you're called to it?
- How does the way you speak reflect your identity as a daughter of God? How about the way you think?
- In what circumstances do you feel uncomfortable acting on your faith? Ask the Holy Spirit to guide you in these situations. Trust that you are never alone.

• • • • • • • • • • • • • • • • • •

PRAY

God, my Father and Lord, have mercy on me when I cave to the ways of the world that seem easier or more convenient than following you. Help me to set my heart on heaven, and give me the strength and courage to live my way closer to that goal in your service each day.

• • • • • • • • • • • • • • • • • •

CALL ON THE COMMUNION OF SAINTS

St. Gianna Beretta Molla is a saint for our time (really—she passed from this world in 1962!). Wife, mother, and doctor, she was diagnosed with a tumor in her uterus while she was pregnant. Doctors suggested she undergo a hysterectomy, which would have saved her life but ended her child's. She refused. St. Gianna made the ultimate sacrifice for a daughter who is still alive today.

St. Gianna Beretta Molla, pray for us!

NINE

ON SPEAKING
WITH CHARITY

BE NICE TO HER

Little kids don't have the verbal filters we expect adults to have. If a child is thinking it, he's saying it. Henry once turned to an eighty-year-old man behind us at a baseball game and said, "Your skin has wrinkles." Another time, with a big smile, he called our pastor "Doody Pants" to his face. Fr. Richard didn't bat an eye, but I still died a little inside.

It can be hard not to feel responsible when your child publically announces something painfully honest, even when everyone knows he doesn't mean to cause any harm. So far, thank God, these incidents have happened with folks who can laugh it off. Jacob, honest and straightforward as he is, took my parents and mother-in-law on a tour of his pre-K classroom during a Grandparents' Day celebration. I remained in the auditorium, cleaning up the reception, believing that he was proudly showing them around his tiny chairs and construction-paper creations. A short time later the adults were back without him, recovering from a collective case of giggles. Jacob was very sweet, they told me, until he thought they'd seen enough and he was ready to get back to his business. "You can go now," he told them. Gee, thanks.

The best, though, was when Henry snuggled up to me at nap time one day and told me he loved me the best. Jacob had repeatedly told me I was on the bottom rung of his family favorites—Daddy and baby sister tied for first, brother came in second, and I was dead last—so this was a big deal. I asked Henry why he felt that way. My love language is words of affirmation, and I expected to have something to cling to in the inevitably challenging moments of the days ahead.

"Jacob loves Daddy more. Someone has to love you the best." Pity from a three-year-old. Awesome.

What we say face-to-face can have a powerful effect, but what we overhear someone say about us can have an even greater effect, for better or for worse. When my oldest was still little, a friend offered me this wisdom about my children: She told me to let them overhear me saying good things about them. Sometimes, the kids do drive me up a wall, but they don't need to hear me complaining to another mom about it, even if she can relate. When I'm at a playdate and the conversation turns to what this one's doing now or how that one is pushing me to my limits, I've been guilty of playing the one-up game. "Oh, I know what you mean. My son . . ."

It is no use to lament behaviors that are currently bugging me. The time to vent is not when little ones are within hearing distance. They are aware of more than we often give them credit for. Without being prideful or dishonest, I try to choose instead to speak of my children's generous moments and of the times they were funny, without making jokes at someone else's expense. It does me good to focus more on those moments, and it builds up their understanding of my love for them. I may even move up a step on Jacob's ladder of love.

Recently, I heard my husband catching up with a friend on the phone in the next room. I was working on something and not intentionally eavesdropping, but bits of his conversation filtered through. He was telling our friend about this book and about the marathon I had signed up for later in the year. He wasn't bragging, but there was a sense of pride in his voice that I welcomed. Rather than complaining about the challenge of incorporating these time-consuming endeavors into our already busy schedule, he expressed them as things that were genuinely good for me, and he was as excited about them as I was. He'd told me the same things to my face, but it meant more when I heard him sharing it with someone else.

Speaking with charity benefits both the speaker and the listener. My thoughts, words, and actions are all connected. So when I dwell on the more frustrating moments of my life, I'm focusing on those as the norm. If I choose to see and express the more joyful, loving, and hopeful moments—without pretending the other stuff doesn't exist—recollections of these will inform how I live my life. I can be more forgiving, more compassionate. This is how I want my Father to see me: to forget the sins he has forgiven and Jesus died for and instead to remember how I've tried to live my life faithfully. This petition is even worked into the Mass: at the sign of peace, the priest prays, "Look not on our sins, but on the faith of your Church, and grant us the peace and unity of your kingdom where you live for ever and ever."

There's a lot I could complain about in the world. My words are a gift I would better use to lift others up, to formulate solutions, and to contribute to building the kingdom of God.

We often play a game at dinner called "High, Low, Surprise," which is based on an Ignatian reflection tool. The concept is self-explanatory. Each person has a turn to cite the best thing of the day, the saddest or worst thing of the day, and something that surprised him or her. For example, "My high was that it was my friend's birthday at school and I got to have a cupcake. My low was that it took a long time to clean up. My surprise is that we're having pizza for dinner!" Doing this at the evening meal means food plays a prominent role in many of our reflections.

When I can, I try to use "High, Low, Surprise" as a way to incorporate something good one of the kids did into conversation. I can see the positive effects on my boys when they hear me say that something one of them did for me was the best thing that happened to me all day. It's also a good time for me to work in something about John. It's important for the kids to know that Daddy and Mommy love each other and take care of each other. We show that as best we can. Putting it into words helps ensure that the kids (and John and I) are conscious of the prominence the marriage has in the life of the family. It's the foundation of our little unit and something John and I need to care for, in order to support our family as a whole.

I can't just speak with charity; I need to listen with charity as well. Too often, I have seen someone's achievement or gift on social media and felt lesser because of it. I hear about someone experiencing something differently than I did and wonder if I've made a mistake. I have caused myself pain by taking things personally that were never meant to be that way.

Jacob was born via induction. He was late; he was big. It was the right choice for us. A "natural" birth (which can mean such a range of things) was never my plan. But when I heard other new moms talking about their totally unmedicated deliveries, I second-guessed myself. Had I somehow failed to give my child enough of myself?

To John, this was silly. In his mind, we made a decision based on the information we had, and everyone turned out well and thriving. Jacob was more than nine pounds at birth. I am five foot three and of average build. Not to get too graphic, but my doctor made a note in my chart for my next delivery: "Tight fit."

It was in the midst of a playdate that I heard a friend of a friend relating her long, painful, unmedicated labor story. There was clearly pride in what she'd done, and birthing a child is always good news. But something didn't sit right with me. Was she being prideful, and was my bristling a result of that, or was the inadequacy I was feeling at hearing her story rooted in my own insecurity?

A week or so later, I was still feeling down about it. Without me mentioning a name or when the conversation took place, another new mom who'd been at the same playdate remembered the conversation I was talking about and talked me down from my feelings of inferiority. Maybe she was being a little prouder than truly necessary, but it had no bearing on my situation, my family, or my choices. I had done what was right for me, and she for her, and it was all worthy of celebration. We had healthy babies, praise God!

In future interactions, the mother with the labor story was always kind to me, especially after our miscarriage. I shrugged the other incident off and tried to let it go. It wasn't until two years later that I learned she had struggled with a serious case of postpartum depression after that delivery. My impression of her turned on its head. I was humbled, to say the least. Perhaps the success of that delivery was a positive note she could hold on to when everything else wasn't turning out how she expected. Her story was never about me. I didn't hear the struggle in her story because I let myself get in the way.

In my writers' critique group, we often talk about how what's not expressed in dialogue is as important as what is. In real life, we don't always answer each other's questions directly. We talk over each other. We speak in fragments. We don't make an effort to use perfect grammar (though sometimes I wish we did). We leave out key details—and only sometimes on purpose. These imperfections and incompletions express the complexities of who we are individually and in relationship with one another. We bring a lot of baggage to our everyday interactions. Only God knows what's really going on in the human heart.

How I choose to speak is just that—a choice. When I ask the Holy Spirit to guide me to use my voice to serve the kingdom, when I recognize and consciously acknowledge that yes, each word I say really does matter, I speak more kindly, more gently, and with greater love. That's good for my soul, good for my family, and good for the little ears that might be listening down the hall.

· · · · · · · · · · · · · · · · · · ·

REFLECT

- When do you find it most challenging to speak with charity? How else could you manage your inconveniences, without using hurtful language?
- Do you always speak about others the way you would if they were present?

- What traits or behaviors bother you most in other people? Might it be that these are things you are particularly susceptible to yourself?

• • • • • • • • • • • • • • • • • • •

PRAY

Dear Lord, God of charity and grace, help me to use my language to serve you today. Help me to see how my thoughts, words, and actions are all connected, and guide me to become a woman of greater integrity and generosity.

• • • • • • • • • • • • • • • • • • •

CALL ON THE COMMUNION OF SAINTS

We learn about Sts. Simeon and Anna in Luke's account of Jesus' presentation in the Temple (see Luke 2:22–38). Both faithful individuals, Simeon and Anna possessed such purity of heart and mind that they quickly recognized the child Jesus as God. In response, they offered their prayer for him and his family, proclaiming the Good News without fear or hesitation. Their proclamation is so important that the Canticle of Simeon is an element of Night Prayer of the Divine Office.

Sts. Simeon and Anna, pray for us.

TEN

ON FRATERNAL/SORORAL CORRECTION

YOU KNOW, SHE LOOKS UP TO YOU

Jacob is the joyful poster child for the tendencies of the oldest child's birth order. He always wants to make plans and sort out logistics, like how we're going to get his karate uniform clean for his practice session three days from now. When he was just two and we brought Henry home, he reveled in helping to care for his little brother, throwing out diapers, showing him how to crawl, and sitting on top of him as if he were a horse. Wait, scratch that last one.

Henry was a classic middle child even before Sarah was born. He is a delightful goofball, who takes full advantage of the fact that his little sister will do whatever he does, whether it's making a super loud sound, banging a cup on the table, or climbing on a structure made of pillows. Even Jacob is susceptible to Henry's ideas. When he was younger, we had to remind Jacob that Henry's supposed to look up to him, not the other way around. And now, we try to show Henry how much Sarah looks up to him and convince him to use this force for good and not only unbridled silliness.

I am the second and youngest child in my family. I don't even have younger cousins, so I didn't hear, "You know, she looks up to you," or feel that pressure growing up. Now that I use it with my boys, even I get bummed out about it sometimes. I feel for them when they want to be silly, but there's someone younger who's bound to parrot their actions. I can see them feel a little stifled, restricted from having what otherwise might be a bit of fun, for fear of influencing someone else who's not ready to make certain behavioral distinctions. Like it or not, it's a responsibility they have.

There are other times, of course, when the behavior is a bad idea for anyone. Then I hope that reminding them they're giving their younger sibling ideas will tap into their love of the other, to motivate the boys in a way that the simple satisfaction of listening to a parent just can't do.

When we're adults, we're supposed to be free from the influences of peer pressure and able to make decisions totally on our own. Let's be honest; that's not how we function as human beings. What we see, read, and hear makes a mark on us. I once read about a study that showed how people subconsciously mimicked the sentence structures of the last thing they read or heard before sitting down to write.[9] Though it wasn't an intentional decision, the material had an impact.

There are forces in my corner of the world that play on me in more dramatic ways than influencing my sentence structure, ways I am not always conscious of. A seemingly insignificant and offhand comment—not even about me—can get my wheels turning in a bad way. It could be something I overheard at a school drop-off. It might be something I read on social media.

Or maybe it's something I discussed with a friend. Especially when I'm tired or worried about something else, I search for implications that don't exist, or at least don't directly involve me. I see outside concerns too immediately through only my own lens, and I let my perceptions affect the way I approach the rest of my day. I know I am not nearly as detached from this world as I'd like to be.

It's tough to get there when, as a mom of little ones, I am so much in the thick of earthly things—laundry, food, toys, books, school, lessons, and caring for a house and a car. I can forget that God is in all these things. In fact, he is the reason these responsibilities are on my plate. They are the realities of my vocation and the ways by which I am called to serve him, through my family. It is through these things that I might be that force of change—for better or for worse—in someone else's life.

Relativism pervades our culture, making it easy for me to think that I can handle something borderline sinful. *It's okay for me*, I think, *because I won't take it to a dangerous place.* I can handle temptation—watching that movie I know has some graphic scenes or bad language, or virtual window shopping when I don't really need anything—because I have my spiritual ducks in a row. It is pride to deny that engaging in these activities will have absolutely no effect on me.

In the Lord's Prayer, we beg our Father to "lead us not into temptation" and to "deliver us from evil." That means all temptation, all evil, not just the stuff that's really bad and that I know I can't handle on my own. Sin usually takes hold little by little, rather than all at once. And not just on me. Unless I live as a desert hermit, my actions will have some kind of impact on my community (and really, they would even as a hermit too). What I mean to do or don't mean to do isn't always the same as what other people see. And either way, it's still making an impact on the core of who I am, even if I can't see it right away. To put it simply, I have a responsibility to myself and to my community to behave in a way that honors the gifts of my life and theirs.

The fact that the phrase "you do you" has become part of our vernacular is proof that our culture has lost appreciation for—perhaps even understanding of—fraternal correction. We are each supposed to be able to do what we feel is right for ourselves, without repercussions. But none of us is that insulated, not in childhood and not in adulthood. And few of us, I would argue, are universally virtuous.

It might be socially acceptable to correct something we see in another if we're really close to that person. I think most people would say that a true friend can and should call you out when you're out of line. But do we do that, even then? Do we know how?

In high school I was reaching a point of stress with everything on my plate. My sarcasm got to a point where it wasn't funny anymore and was starting to get just mean. That's all my best friend had to say, that I was starting to get mean. It stung to hear it, but I knew she was only acknowledging something she knew I could do better, that something was keeping me from being the best version of myself. I started to watch my language, to pay more attention to what I was saying and at whose expense. I was starting to see the problem myself before she said something, but no one had complained. I wasn't sure if it was in my head. Maybe I didn't want to admit that I could be that hurtful. But I can, and I was. And with a carefully timed word by one of the people who knows me best in this world, I found the courage and the motivation to change. I don't know whether I have ever been that person for someone else, but I hope I have if it was needed.

The influence of the people we love and respect goes the other way too. There have been times when I've had an impact on people around me, without even realizing it. Talking to my then boyfriend, now husband, on the phone one evening in college, I learned that he'd chosen to spend his post-Katrina spring break in service because he'd seen me do the same. I served because I felt called to (and a lot of my friends were going), not because I was trying to motivate John to do something. But it stirred a desire to serve in him, which then rippled to do good for people who were suffering whom I would never even meet.

The *Catechism* goes so far as to say that charity "demands . . . fraternal correction" (*CCC*, 1829), so we can be sure that when done properly, the act is not bossy but generous. A gentle admonition from someone we trust can motivate us in a way we can't do for ourselves. Sinful as we are, humans are more likely to do something that requires sacrifice when it's for someone else, rather than for themselves. I read about another study in which signs were posted in a hospital asking people to use hand sanitizer to stop the spread of germs. More people used the gel when the accompanying sign noted the benefits to other people than when the plea was made to preserve one's own health.[10] I always find that I struggle less to give up a food or habit for Lent when it's a sacrifice to offer our Lord than when I try to do it on my own simply because it would be a healthier or wiser choice. I need a stronger sense of motivation than to better myself. Because aren't I already fine as I am?

Fraternal or sororal correction must always come from a place of great love and humility. It's never about telling someone else she's wrong and I'm right. It has to come from a place of compassion and understanding, of wanting the good of the other, regardless of what it means for me. That said, the first step must always be to check my own relationship with God. Do I acknowledge that he is in control and I am not? Do I recognize my own sinfulness, and am I working to improve the areas I'm struggling with? Who am I looking up to as a role model? A celebrity? A successful writer? Another mom I only know superficially? Or the saints?

Only if I am on the journey to being "perfect, just as [my] heavenly Father is perfect" (Mt 5:48), and only if I know that I'm not there yet, is it possible that my attempt at correction will do any good at all.

Sometimes speaking up for what's right can come across as being pompous, self-righteous, or holier-than-thou. But if it comes from the right place and it's rooted in humility, I think holding each other accountable could move mountains in our society—starting in our homes.

Jesus didn't ask us to only not do bad things. He implored us to do good, to do right. There was a commercial a few years ago, where one person's good deed led to another and another. I was inspired by that thirty-second spot to find a way to take a moment out of my day for someone else. Our right and just works can easily do the same and encourage the people around us to make some small sacrifice that will ripple out to a more peaceful world. This is how our children learn from us. Even as adults, this modeling is often how we learn from each other.

A religious sister in my parish spent much of her upbringing in Portugal and has a strong devotion to Our Lady of Fatima. Speaking to our moms group one evening, she told us that no matter what else she includes in her Rosary intentions, she always includes peace, per Our Lady's request. That stuck with me, and I started to do the same. I recalled the words of a hymn, "Let peace begin with me, / Let this be the moment now." If we truly want peace on earth, why not have it start now, with us? The question is, where does it start?

I think it starts in being humble and gracious enough to give and receive criticism when it is merited. Someday, Jesus is going to call us out on everything. All that we thought was in darkness will come to light. How much better to step into the light now with the help of our brothers and sisters and as a good example to our children? They won't know how to speak up for what's right if they don't see it happening. There is a cost, to be sure. But there is a reward, too, and it will be great in heaven.

Peace could begin on earth, right now, with me.

• •

REFLECT

- When did you see sin in someone you loved but didn't speak up about it? What prevented you from doing so? How could you do differently in the future?
- Has anyone called you out on something that led to positive change? What about that experience compelled you to do something differently?
- In what area of your life are you setting a poor example for others? How have you seen this manifest, and what can you do about it today?

• • • • • • • • • • • • • • • • • •

PRAY

Lord of all, you gave your children family, school, church, and civil communities to live in. Help us to be grateful for these communities, recognizing our contemporaries as fellow sojourners toward you, toward Truth. Guide us to walk together, correcting faults where they lie, so that ours might be a more peaceful world.

• • • • • • • • • • • • • • • • • •

CALL ON THE COMMUNION OF SAINTS

In her apparitions to the three children of Fatima—Sts. Jacinta and Francisco and Bl. Lucia—Our Lady foretold future political happenings in our world. She encouraged the children, and by extension all of us, to pray the Rosary daily. Her miracle of the dancing sun is further evidence that the spiritual and secular worlds are not separate entities but two sides of the same coin.

Our Lady of Fatima, pray for us.

ELEVEN

ON CONFESSION AND FORGIVENESS

YOU NEED TO SAY "I'M SORRY"

I try not to get involved every time my kids fight about something. For one thing, they need to learn to work things out among themselves. For another, I don't think I have the stamina, and it's nice to have a hot meal now and then.

When I do step in, I'll ask one kid what happened. What I inevitably get first is a litany of the other child's transgressions. "Okay," I'll say. "That was wrong. Now, what were you doing while this was happening?" I am usually met with a sheepish expression or some suggestion that he forgot what he was doing. "You need to say 'I'm sorry,'" I remind my little one. Even at such a young age, it is much easier to see what someone else did wrong than to acknowledge the errors of our own ways.

I get it. It's tough to admit that we've messed up. Sometimes we just aren't aware of the injury we've caused another. Our pride can be stronger than our humility, which isn't often celebrated these days. To many, it looks like weakness. This may be the way of the world, but it's not the way of Christianity. Scripture tells us God rejoices more over one repentant sinner than over ninety-nine righteous men. It is when we are weak that we can welcome the grace to be strong in Christ Jesus.

I'm not very good at Confession. I've had some bad experiences. Once, I guess I was way too vague, because the priest told me there wasn't a sin in what I'd confessed; there was nothing he could absolve me from. Another time, I went in part to seek advice about something I was wrestling with. I left the sacrament in tears, and not the good kind. In retrospect, the answer was honest, but it was presented harshly.

It bugs me to no end when one of the kids throws a casual "sorry" over his shoulder after making a poor judgment call. It doesn't go deep enough. Instead, we teach them to stop what they're doing, put down anything in their hands, and stand up straight with their hands together. They are to wait for an opportunity to get the other's attention and make their apology while looking the other in the eye. The kids know they are to say the other person's name and what exactly it is they're sorry for. I'm not sure where I got this from, or what stirred it in me, but it's the way we do things now. Getting them to do it this way, to really stop and face the other, can be tedious. When it feels that way, I remember that there is a long-term as well as a short-term goal in progress. We are preparing them for a sacrament, something I hope they will have an easier time with than I do.

In the course of teaching them this method of making amends, I found myself saying things that I really needed to hear, things that I didn't even realize were lacking in myself: "Why do you think what you did was wrong? How did it hurt?" or "Sorry means you're going to try not to do it again." Is that honestly the way I approach Confession? Doesn't never committing my sins again in the future seem nearly impossible?

I know my faults (some of them), and I know I'm called to be perfect as my Father is perfect (see Matthew 5:48). But most of the time, I don't really believe it's going to happen. I know how hard it is for me to avoid certain sins, and I don't always have hope that I'm going to be able to stop those things for good. I'm afraid of what things would look like if I did. It would involve a radical change, something I can't see sticking.

But then, I am not called to make any change of this sort on my own. I don't go to Confession as a way to earn points that turn into advanced powers, like in a video game where, if you earn enough coins, you'll get to throw fireballs for a limited time, at least until you mess up again.

In high school, on the same retreat where I was called to live out loud and be countercultural, a young man spoke about his experience with Confession. He said that in preparing to receive the sacrament, he understood that he was already forgiven before he stepped into the confessional. That didn't negate his needing to follow through, to make the sacrifice of his time and pride to confess his sins out loud and complete the penance given him. But he recognized that he wasn't supposed to be doing those things alone. The whole thing was about recognizing God was already with him, that God had been with him the whole time. It was about decreasing himself, so that God might increase in him. It was about surrender.

My father-in-law is an amazing man. (You don't hear that every day, do you?) He has a congenital joint condition that has rendered him homebound. The basic movements I typically take for granted—unless I'm in the third trimester of a pregnancy—are extremely painful for him. He has every reason to be a curmudgeon, to shake his fist at God, and to be bitter about the way he's living. But if he complains, it's usually on the tail end of a joke. When I met him fourteen years ago, he could get around pretty well with a crutch and cane. I often found him in his wheelchair at the head of the table, cracking jokes or trying to get us to play one more round of poker or Pictionary. His life is largely devoted to prayer and spiritual reading (and fantasy football, when it's that time of year). He loves me like his own daughter, and I love him like a second father.

Humility is nothing new to him. He has to ask for help for most everything physical these days. While he was more active when his six kids were young—swimming in the backyard pool; boating on vacation; and making trips to Dunkin' Donuts, his self-proclaimed shrine, for a "coffee, extra light and sweet, and whatever you want"—there have always been things that he couldn't do. It hasn't been easy for him. But he is joyful. He is funny. He has hope and faith like I've never seen.

My husband has told me that one of the most influential things about his father as he was growing up was his willingness to say he was sorry. As an adult, the importance he continues to place on a legitimate apology remains a profound thing. On the rare occasion he has been a little cranky when I stopped over or got too upset about one of those board games, I received a heartfelt, honest, look-you-in-the-eye apology in twenty-four hours or less. Included is a direct request for forgiveness, which of course is always warmly granted.

I have tried to make the same gesture a habit with my kids, apologizing when I've yelled too much or made a false assumption about who had that sword/gun/fishing pole/leaf blower first. I've included asking for forgiveness from God and the grace to be a better mom the next day in our nighttime prayers, to model this kind of petition. Rookie mistake: with kids this little, getting too specific has backfired. Rather than pray for his own conversion of heart, Jacob once prayed that I would be a better mommy the next day. Ouch.

My father-in-law's faith life is very active. He lives by the sacraments. He receives daily Communion, which my mother-in-law brings to him. He receives the sacrament of Confession every week in our home. I strive for daily Mass attendance, but my personal best for Confession is once a month, and that inevitably falls by the wayside when we hit a streak of busy Saturday afternoons.

What a difference it makes when I go regularly, when I think of reconciliation not as a cure or a Band-Aid to something that's bugging me but as a vitamin, a supplement to take regularly in order to become who I am called to be. I am more patient, kinder, and slower to anger. I give and receive love more fully and more easily when I am aware of how completely and unreservedly it's been offered to me.

My sons share a nebulizer for respiratory issues, especially in the winter. One of the medications we have is a rescue drug, which is intended to be used when coughing has gotten too frequent and disruptive. The other is a maintenance drug, which they also have in their inhalers to use on a more regular basis. This is about keeping things in check before they go too far down the road that has, thank God only once, landed us in the hospital.

It is easier to live my faith, no matter the circumstances, when I treat Confession like a maintenance drug rather than a rescue medication, when I make saying "I'm sorry" part of my regular life, instead of relying on it only in situations I perceive to be emergencies.

It's then that I realize how much I need God, how little of my own conversion and life of faith I'm supposed to come up with on my own. God wants me to be willing and able to say

I'm sorry. He has a special time and place to call me to it. I am to accept the will of God in my life but also to let him guide me, to lean on the Holy Spirit to give me the words to speak, to beg the Virgin Mary to intercede for me to her son.

In college I read Fr. Henri Nouwen's meditations in *The Return of the Prodigal Son* (any surprise our son's name is Henry?) on the life-changing consequences of reclaiming one's "sonship" or "daughtership," as the case may be. The biggest movement in the prodigal son's life, Fr. Nouwen suggests, is not when he falls at his father's feet and begs forgiveness. It's way before that. He essentially wished his father dead in asking for his inheritance and then blew it, as if to say the life his father had worked to build didn't matter. He knows he's not worthy to come back to the place he left behind. But eventually he remembers and accepts that he is this man's son and that he was promised there would always be a place for him. When he starts to trust in that, when he turns his eyes back toward home, that's when the magic—or rather, the conversion—happens. His father runs to him, delighted to see him again. He is forgiven before he speaks a single word.

This echoes the message I heard on that high school retreat and that I'm trying to teach my kids and myself. Confession shouldn't be a scary thing. Of course I should strive to make a good confession, which would come more easily as the result of a regular examination of conscience. But getting the wording right isn't really what it's about. It's about the movement of my heart back to God. The more regularly I make that movement, the more natural it becomes. It's spiritual muscle memory. It might feel awkward at first, but that's because I'm stretching new things, muscles I didn't even know I had. The more I use them, the stronger they become. But still, my strength lies only in him. The strength I am building up is the ability to fall into his arms.

• • • • • • • • • • • • • • • • • • •

REFLECT

- When was the last time you went to Confession? What's preventing you from going back?
- Where is an area in your life that has created distance between you and God? What are you clinging to? How is it manifesting itself in sin, and how might letting go change your relationship with the Lord?
- Is there someone in your life you need to apologize to? Your kids, a family member, a friend, or yourself? What do you have to lose by apologizing? By not apologizing?

• • • • • • • • • • • • • • • • • • •

PRAY

God my Father, you know what we need before we ask for it. Help us to lean on you in all things, especially in the sins we don't really believe we can stop committing. Through the sacrament of Confession, grant us grace, courage, and a conversion of heart so that we can lean more completely on you and your forgiveness.

● ● ● ● ● ● ● ● ● ● ● ● ● ● ● ● ● ● ●

CALL ON THE COMMUNION OF SAINTS

St. John Vianney (aka the Cure of Ars) struggled to become a priest. Book learning wasn't his thing, but he possessed tremendous piety and faithfulness. He served as a parish priest in the small French town of Ars. Though the town's population was only just over two hundred people, he came to spend up to sixteen hours a day hearing confessions. People traveled great distances to experience the healing power of reconciliation through his humble—and necessary—ministry.

St. John Vianney, pray for us.

TWELVE

ON THE BLESSED VIRGIN AS OUR MOTHER

IT'S OKAY; MOMMY'S HERE

I love the excitement I see in my kids when they spot Daddy out the window, walking home from the train. Toys are dropped, projects are halted, and a mad rush to the door ensues. I feel the same way, although my "Thank God you're home!" generally has a hint of desperation in it as well.

Even though John ranks a couple of spots above me as far as Jacob's concerned, I know there are times for all the kids when only Mommy will do. For a child, a bonk on the head, an argument with a sibling, or simply being too tired can feel like the end of the world. Sometimes it takes a snuggle and a song. Other times, a look of sympathy and a kiss blown across the room will do.

We mothers are built to protect our children, to have a sense, whether it's instinct or impulses learned in the proverbial trenches of childcare, of what they need and how to deliver it. It is a wonderful feeling to have a child relax in your arms, to have him stop crying and find peace curled up against your heart.

The feeling of wanting my own mother hasn't gone away as I've become an adult. I'm lucky that we started our family in Brooklyn when she was just a little more than an hour away in New Jersey. About four years into our marriage, we moved back to our hometown. For a while, she was only six minutes away by car.

My mom has been by my side through everything. When I was younger and we had one of those here's-what-you-don't-do-at-parties talks (rendered irrelevant by my never going to those parties but rather sewing and baking with equally tame friends on Friday nights instead), she ended it by saying, "But no matter what happens, you can always call me, and I will come get you. No matter what."

It's still true. When I called her and said simply, "We lost our baby," her response was, "I'll be right there." Before I knew it, she and my dad were at the door. They must have flown to have made the time they did. She or my dad called me every day after for weeks, just to see how I was doing. Sometimes we talked about the baby, other times about something funny Jacob did. It didn't matter what we talked about. I heard her voice. I knew she was there.

Living in the same state, we see each other all the time. She comes over to watch the kids while I work out, or we run errands together. My kids are growing up with this wonderful, unlikely experience of potentially seeing both sets of grandparents on any old day, just because someone stopped by. They know in a personal and everyday way the love of their mother and their two grandmothers. Add in the love of the Blessed Mother, and their maternal love tank is overflowing.

I didn't understand the Blessed Virgin super well growing up. Jesus' mama? Okay, I'll take it. Born without sin? I can't imagine that, but okay, I'm still with you. We pray for her intercession but don't worship her, obviously—we only worship God. I could understand that. Still, she seemed distant. I couldn't relate to her. When she was a teenager, she birthed the Son of God in a stable. At that age, I was playing field hockey at a high school in New Jersey, still learning to take care of myself. What did I have in common with this woman who lived a radically different life two thousand years ago?

When I was pregnant the first time, I was excited, but I needed some help negotiating the spiritual aspect of growing a person in my womb. In a lot of ways, that experience is beautiful, but to quote my own mother, it can also be kind of like that movie *Aliens*, where someone is living inside of you and eating all your food.

Through the majority of my pregnancy with Jacob, we lived in Manhattan and were members of a parish on the Upper East Side, where we were the youngest parishioners by decades. The priests there were kind and welcoming to us. When I asked one of them for recommendations on what to read as an expectant mother, he was apologetic about not having much to offer me. He didn't know of any books, per se, but he did offer me the Nativity narratives of the Gospel.

Jacob was born in the fall, so I didn't experience Advent or Christmas large with child. I was used to relegating these readings to that time of year. But as I looked to them during my pregnancy, I finally found something I could relate to in Mary. In our bodies, in the temporal, we shared the experience of pregnancy. She rode a donkey nine months pregnant. I made a horrible subway transfer at Fifty-First Street in the hottest summer on record. It is miserable to sweat before you even get to work. But it had to be done. It wasn't about me; it was a sacrifice I made for my child. I was starting to understand Mary.

The particulars of my deliveries and the early months of my children's lives are different than Mary's experience. But the basic experience is the same: the total gift of your heart to someone else, the feeling of that warm bundle of life resting in your arms, the peacefulness of a well-fed and content little boy, and the satisfaction of offering him what he needs.

Parenting isn't all roses and butterflies, of course. As the kids grow, I continue to try to relate my experience to the Blessed Mother's. Sometimes it is in anger, I admit. *She only had one, and he was without sin!* I think. The other side of that, of course, is that she got frustrated too. Human emotions were not foreign to her. But she found a way to deal with them that wasn't sinful. It must be possible for me to do the same. Somehow.

Sometimes I wondered if Jesus was colicky, even though—praise God—mine so far have not been. When ten-month-old Jacob was diagnosed with food allergies to four of the top eight allergens, I wondered if Jesus had food allergies. Probably not, but was he nearsighted? Did he get sick often as a kid? Did he ever sprain an ankle or skin a knee?

My favorite moments of the movie *The Passion of the Christ* are those between Jesus and his mother. In one instance, she calls him to lunch and he shows her the set of table and chairs he's been working on. They make jokes, they laugh together, and he kisses her with affection. Later we see the urgency with which John leads Mary to a place where she can see Jesus on his road to Calvary. There is deep pain in her expression. She aches as if someone has ripped her own heart from her chest.

This is what it feels like when our children suffer. Just before he was two, Jacob had an allergic reaction that required an ambulance ride to the hospital. His little body was covered, just covered, in hives. He was miserable; it was difficult to see him lethargic and clingy. I thought the food I'd bought for him was safe, but it wasn't. The four hours it took for the reaction to clear up felt like an eternity, but eventually he was bouncing around again, singing, smiling, and back to his beautiful self.

It may not be another allergic reaction that causes him pain in the future. It could be a harsh word on the playground, a failed attempt to break a board at karate, or a bad stomach flu. When I start to consider the possibilities for pain in this world, I see they are endless. It is unlikely that I will always physically be there for him and our other children, but I hope I will be around for a long time. My maternal grandmother lived to ninety-eight, so perhaps genes are on my side. Either way, I am making an effort to teach my children that they have another mother in addition to me, their two grandmothers, and their godmothers.

On the Cross, Jesus gave us his mother as our Mother. As a family, we pray for her intercession every day, and even more often when the kids have trouble falling asleep or are hurting in one way or another. We offer a Rosary on the way to school in the morning. We say the Angelus or Regina Caeli before lunch. We have her image around the house. We are learning, together, to appreciate her beauty and celebrate her feast days.

Consecrating myself to Mary has made a colossal difference in my stress levels. The more I entrust to Mary, the less I have to carry on my own. She gave herself to God completely in her *fiat*, and she guides me to do the same. When we lost Ethan, I turned to Mary. She, too, lost a son. As mediatrix of graces, Mother Mary need only be asked to intercede for us. As a mother, she understands in that particular way the emotions and challenges of devoting yourself, mind, body, and soul, to another.

When my grandmother was sick, I noticed she kept a rosary near her. She wasn't an openly prayerful woman, but I knew from talking with her at the end of her life that she knew whose she was and where she wanted to go. She talked not of passing but of going home. Decades before, she had chosen Mary as her confirmation name. And the last time I saw her, the morning of her funeral, there was a rosary in her hands, per tradition.

As my own mother lived those days taking care of her, making decisions with her sister, and hurting for the loss of the woman she still called Mommy, she was never far from her rosary either. They didn't talk about this with me as much as they showed me where they went when things got tough—to their Mother. The more I do the same, the closer I come, too, to her son, and the better I can serve him as the mother, the woman, and the daughter he created me to be.

In that Manhattan apartment, when I was first getting to know Mary, John and I had kept a porcelain figure of Our Lady, a family heirloom passed down from my great-grandparents, on our dresser. When John brought me flowers, he put most of them in a vase on the dining table, the focal point of our living space and an area that got a good deal of sunlight. He also put one in a glass on the dresser for Our Lady. Despite our bedroom being much darker, that flower always bloomed a little longer. Even before I knew how much I needed her, Mother Mary was there for me.

• • • • • • • • • • • • • • • • • • • •

REFLECT

- Has your relationship with Mary changed since you became a mother? What virtue do you feel called to grow in now that she might help with?
- Many of the saints have had special devotions to Mary. Consider the example of St. John Paul II, St. Louis de Montfort, or St. Elizabeth Ann Seton. What can you learn from their *fiat*?
- How does Mary fit into your everyday prayer life? Learn a new Marian prayer (the Rosary, the Angelus, or the Memorare) and try incorporating it into your life for a week. Keep an eye out for a change in your spirit.

• • • • • • • • • • • • • • • • • • • •

PRAY

Lord Jesus, you gave us your Mother as our own. Thank you for the gift of a faithful woman's example of love and sacrifice. Bless our homes, through her intercession, with her peacefulness and gentleness.

• • • • • • • • • • • • • • • • • • • •

CALL ON THE COMMUNION OF SAINTS

Mary is the Mother of Jesus and the Mother of us all. We've already invoked her intercession twice in these pages, but she is so much for us, I can't help but include her again. Mothers know a special tenderness for their children, and Mary has this in spades for each and every one of us. She loves us unconditionally and, as the mediatrix of all graces, she intercedes for us before her son. Whatever you need, whenever you need it, Mother Mary's your girl.

Holy Mary, Mother of God, pray for us.

THIRTEEN

ON RELYING ON GOD

YOU'RE NOT BIG ENOUGH
TO DO THAT ALONE

The first time I watched *Finding Nemo* as a parent, I cringed in the final scenes. For the uninitiated, Marlin, Nemo's father, is super protective of his son. His undersea helicopter parenting is reasonable, seeing as he lost his wife and their hundreds of other children to a predator when Nemo was still in his egg. But Nemo is older now, and ready for an adventure. He gives in to peer pressure on his first day of school, wanting to prove that his "lucky fin," one damaged in the attack, doesn't slow him down. Marlin reprimands him without letting Nemo get a word in, and Nemo's had enough. In an act of defiance, he swims farther away from safety than he should and is captured by—of all people—a dentist.

The rest of the film is Marlin's search through the ocean for his son. He is frantic; he feels he's failed; and he's lost the one thing left in the world that gives his life meaning. It isn't until the end that he realizes the damage was caused by his fear of allowing his son to take risks. At some point, he was going to have to let Nemo go, to let him try things on his own, sometimes succeeding and sometimes failing. He needed to trust that he'd taught his son all he could and that Nemo would make good decisions. But he also had to come to terms with those being his son's decisions. In the movie, even a fish has free will. And even a fish parent struggles to accept that.

I am not much of a risk taker. My happy place is on the couch, feet curled up, writing or knitting or reading, and wrapped up in a big cozy blanket. Tea doesn't hurt. Neither does a hunk of dark chocolate. I don't mind being outside, but I enjoy the feeling of safety and peace I get from being still, when I can manage it.

Toddlers typically don't enjoy the same pastimes. They want to run, jump, climb, and try, try, try. What's new? How can I get up there, in there, and through there? Taking my children to the playground is often an exercise in blood-pressure escalation. I don't want to hover, but I also don't want to see my kids get hurt. I'm supposed to protect them, right?

It's a different story when my husband joins us. He is more confident in what they're capable of. He can take a step back and trust that, yes, he's big enough to do that. He suggests ways to use the equipment that I wouldn't have dared think of. Sometimes, my pulse still races and I opt to just stay home on the aforementioned couch. But when I join them, when I see what the kids are capable of, I'm reminded that they are their own people. They are gifts entrusted to me to guide toward heaven. They are not carbon copies of me, even if our baby pictures do have a good deal in common. They are creatures with bodies, souls, and free will, all of which deserve respect and freedom to stretch.

When my oldest was diagnosed with allergies, on the one hand I figured I had even more reason to keep him close in order to keep him safe. In an instant, I could spot a bag of Goldfish across the busy after-school Brooklyn playground, and I'd keep an eye on the child eating them for the length of our playtime. This may sound extreme, but Jacob once reacted from a kiss after John had milk in his coffee. Another time he and John came home from the playground with a dose of Benadryl already in his system. A child had spilled ice cream on the slide. Jacob went down on his belly and his shirt shifted up. The ice cream touched his skin, and bam! Hives. How would I ever send this child to school? What would happen when a friend invited him to dinner? How would he date? How would he feed his own children, if fatherhood was his vocation?

The questions swirled through my mind, especially after an accident. There have been few, but I remember every one. We'd go a long time without needing cortisone or an antihistamine, and I'd wonder if we were just being really careful or if something had resolved. Then something would happen to prove the former. We needed to be vigilant.

As he's grown, I've noticed things in him that seem built in to protect him. Jacob was never a kid who reached for someone else's food, except maybe once as a baby. He learned to read early and noticed how I read packages in the store and again at home. He was interested in learning how to protect himself and, from an early age, owned this thing that made him different. He is the least picky eater of our children and often tells me, "Mom, this dinner is a keeper!" All these things show me that despite the dangers, he has what he needs to be safe, to be the person God needs him to be.

I want to hold him closer because of the fact that a piece of cheese could give him trouble breathing, but I quickly realized, with the help of our friend Marlin, how problematic and limiting that could be as he grows up. Because of his allergies, I saw earlier than I might have how I need to let him go, how I need to entrust him to God.

They say that all parenthood is a series of moments in which we let go. I thought of that when I gave birth to Jacob. He was no longer inside me. I would never hold him so closely again. Now it was possible for others to hold him, to hear him, and to feel him move. From his first breath, I was letting him go.

If I have to let my children go—and sometimes denial still seems easier than doing so—then I need to let them go with all the best tools, the greatest understanding of their faith, and the most personal relationship with Jesus Christ that I can help build in them. Even when they're grown, I want them to know that in the ways that count, they're never really alone.

I didn't grow up celebrating feast days or baptismal days as my husband did, and as an adult, I became enamored of the liturgical calendar. Despite what the stores tell you, Christmas doesn't start in November, and the music on the radio ought to continue long after 6:00 p.m. on December 25. The weeks leading up to Easter Sunday are not the time for bunnies and chicks but for penance and service. Nor are these days totally dark and dreary. There is a Sunday, a little Easter, you can count on every week as well as a variety of feasts or solemnities thrown in, depending on the year.

There is a rhythm to the Church's life, and it is intended to respect our humanity while drawing us closer to the Lord. I can certainly try to live my life on my own, to follow the tides of culture, to celebrate as I prepare to move on to the next thing as soon as the first is over. Or I can linger in the seasons, breathe them in, and rejoice in the virtues they can draw out in me if I let them. I can trust that the little sacrifices I make build in me the muscles of faith, hope, and courage that I need to lean on the Lord when work gets messy, children misbehave, John and

I don't see eye to eye, and the washing machine starts spewing soap around the laundry room.

All of scripture and the traditions of the Church are God trying to tell me, "You don't have to do this alone. I don't want you to. You can't. Please, let me help." It's different than Marlin's fear of losing control. This is love. This is God asking me to live the life he gave me in the way it was meant to be lived.

I can be the stubborn child who answers, in the words of my daughter, "I got it, Daddy. I got it." Or I can surrender to the Lord who made me, who understands me, and who knows that I am not big enough, strong enough, or wise enough to live this life on my own—not to live it to the fullest, at least. I can muddle through, I can survive, and I may be esteemed in the eyes of my friends and family or even the world. But if I have not love, if I have not surrender to the divine will, I will be like a fish swimming in the wrong direction, not making progress, not getting to where, in my heart of hearts, I know I want to be.

As a mother, it is my job to welcome experiences that can help build my children's self-esteem and sense of worth. The best way I can do that is to show them how to trust in the Lord. When that gets hard to do, I let the rhythm of the calendar guide me. I cling to the sacraments. Like Marlin's sweet friend Dory, I choose to "just keep swimming."

• • • • • • • • • • • • • • • • • • •

REFLECT

- What are you most afraid of in your children's lives? Is there something in your own life that causes or has caused this?

- How much of your life and your family's life are you really, truly willing to hand over to God?
- What do you think might come of relying more completely on your Father?

• • • • • • • • • • • • • • • • • •

PRAY

God my Father, you know every hair on my head, every thought in my mind, and every desire in my heart. Help me to be honest with myself about the things I fear the most and to entrust them to you with my whole heart.

• • • • • • • • • • • • • • • • • •

CALL ON THE COMMUNION OF SAINTS

St. Gerard Majella is recognized as patron of mothers, especially expectant mothers. He is often invoked for a safe and happy delivery, but we needn't forget him after the newborn stage. If submitting your will for your family to God is a challenge, try offering it to St. Gerard as an intermediary. He will carry your prayers to our ever-loving Father with haste.

St. Gerard, pray for us.

FOURTEEN

ON THE COMMUNION OF SAINTS

DO YOU NEED HELP?

A lot of people say toddlers are like tyrants, but mine are better described as control freaks. They want to do it all themselves: the pouring, the opening, the closing, the switching, the button pushing (literal and figurative), and the carrying. My daughter, for instance, loves to be held, and she is fascinated by the dark. Once she succeeds in getting me to pick her up, she often wants to walk through the house turning off the lights. She learned this, of course, from her older brother, the proud owner of a headlamp gifted to him by his godparents. For the record, we have never gone either spelunking or even camping. It's a domestic headlamp.

Sarah also loves to clean things up. She is less interested in whether the thing she's set her sights on needs to be cleaned up or whether the person using the thing is finished with his or her task. She closes drawers while I am reaching for a clean dish to put away. She shuts the garbage can when I turn back to the colander for another shrimp that needs to lose its tail before hitting the frying pan. She cleans up the Legos while Henry's still building his airport truck-repair shop. We tell her to stop when we're not ready yet, but she insists on doing things her own way.

Of course, it's important for kids to try to learn new things, and unless they're feeling particularly stubborn, this often turns into a plea for help. Mother does know best *sometimes*. That bag *is* too heavy. That word *is* too big. That light switch, darn it, *is* too high.

Asking for help is not my strong suit. If you need proof, ask my husband. He could probably write his own book on my sense of pride. I have strict and immovable rules on receiving help. To understand them, you'd have to read my mind. I welcome help only when I ask for it. Oh, well, and also when you're supposed to know I need it but I haven't said a word. It's not fair, I know. I don't get it either sometimes.

A few years ago, we moved in with my in-laws. Jacob wasn't yet three, and Henry was eight months old. My mother-in-law, not named Theresa for nothing, wholehearted servant of God that she is, tried her best to help me right from the start, never mind her caring for her homebound husband, running an in-home daycare, and still mothering her youngest child through her final year of high school. Mama is the most selfless person I have ever met in my entire life. Our community is awed by her patience, her joyfulness, her perseverance, and her courage. I am also particularly fond of her love of disaster movies and the film *What About Bob?*

The point is, she is kind and generous and never, ever puts herself first. She'd fold my laundry when she saw it downstairs. She'd hold the door for me at church. She'd remind me when it was garbage day and even offer to take mine out. And because of all this, I kid you not, I got so mad.

It was help that I hadn't asked for and didn't think I needed. I thought I should probably accept it, but I was afraid that if I did, she would just keep helping me. Heaven forbid! How dare a caring family member try to help a mother of young children care for her house when she's also trying to settle into a new place and work part time from home? I behaved very much like a toddler: "I can do it! Let me! Let me!" I needed to let go of my pride and just say "thank you," instead of following my overzealous and not quite sincere thanks with, "But really, you don't have to do that for me. . . . Please don't do that for me."

Many of us, especially millennial women, were raised to embrace a sense of independence. We were told, time and again, that we could be anything we wanted to be. I am absolutely grateful for the confidence and hopefulness this instilled in me, the knowledge of my dignity as a person and as a woman. However, it seems I missed the memo on the fact that I wasn't likely to get there on my own.

Independent as I can be, I was born into communities, temporal and spiritual. I have family, friends, and, God help me, the internet from which to get advice, research, and anecdotes on every aspect of parenting from a broad range of perspectives. For the most part, this is good. We need hermits and contemplatives among us in this day and age as much as ever, but most people were built to live in community. Humans are social creatures; we thrive on interaction. As mothers, we interact constantly. Everywhere. All the time. Even in circumstances that we used to take for granted as private.

At the same time, there is only so much help I can get from the things and even the people of this world. I was made to spend time here, but my true destination is heaven, to be with my God and Father, who created me with the purpose of sharing his magnificent love. There is a community there, too, one that I can connect with while I'm still here on earth—namely, the Communion of Saints. A community just waiting for my plea for help.

There is a saint for everything. Literally, everything. There's a patron saint of coffee (who also looks out for unattractive people), of movies, of expectant mothers, of travelers, of writers, of children preparing for Communion, of the internet, and even of fireworks. These are souls who, like St. Thérèse of Lisieux declared of herself, "spend [their] heaven doing good on earth." They are my brothers and sisters in Christ, who are at his feet and want to intercede for me. The catch, if there is one, is that their aid is only available if I embrace the humility and the good sense to ask for it.

Many know of St. Anthony of Padua as the go-to for lost items. St. Boniface has a knack for locating parking spaces in seemingly impossible situations. But I think the saints would be pleased if I didn't only come to them when something was wrong. Don't I want more for my children than for them to come to me when they need money or a ride? I want to grow true relationships with them—real, lasting connections, the building of which I know to be my vocation as a mother.

Having a relationship with a saint is the same as making a new friend. You spend time together. You talk, you listen. You get to know the other's history and what's important to him or her. You make this connection because you share some significant value or interest. It lasts because you make it a priority.

I used to think of the saints as I saw them in stained-glass windows: enrobed, halos shining, and beatific smiles on their centuries-old faces. Lately I've been getting to know some pretty amazing modern saints worth considering as well, saints who walked this earth at the same time I, or at least my parents, did: St. John Paul II, St. John XXIII, St. Josemaría Escrivá, St. Gianna Beretta Molla, and St. Teresa of Calcutta, to name only a few. I consider the people dying for their faith around the world, even today, present-day martyrs. I think of the children who don't make it out of the womb. Saints are still in the making today, right now. Faith still lives and breathes and dies for love of the Lord.

As with baptismal days, the feast days of saints relevant to our immediate family result in bonus dessert nights at our house. For Jacob, it's St. James the Greater, St. Paul (who gets two!), and St. John Paul II, whom Jacob claimed on his own, for their shared initials and middle name. Henry celebrates the feast of St. Henry, which is fitting because, like our Henry, the saint is often depicted with a sword. For Sarah Theresa, we celebrate all the great variants of her middle name: St. Teresa of Calcutta, St. Thérèse of Lisieux, and St. Teresa of Avila.

We named our kids with saints in mind, but for a while I struggled to find a saint I could connect with. There is no St. Lindsay, though my parents had me baptized with the understanding of my name as a derivative of Elizabeth. I didn't make a strong connection to St. Elizabeth Ann Seton until I learned we had the same birthday and she was also a mother with a side job, per se. Then I realized that her Daughters of Charity lived by the rule of St. Vincent de Paul, for whom my childhood and current parish is named.

These things may be arbitrary, but they were a way into my learning more about St. Elizabeth. Just like we sometimes need the introduction of a mutual friend to launch the start of a new friendship, I needed something I could relate to, something that felt relevant for me to engage with. The more I learned about St. Elizabeth, the more there was to relate to. She, too, had a particular devotion to the Blessed Mother, though in her case, it was the result of losing her own mother as a young girl. St. Elizabeth didn't grow up in a Catholic household. While my mother passed the faith on to me, it wasn't something our family life was built around. I, too, chose to follow the Church, in my own time and circumstances. The more I learned about the challenges she faced, the more encouragement I found for the trials on my own spiritual journey.

It is my hope that routinely asking for the intercession of the saints in our home will teach my children that they have an extensive community rooting for them and guiding them on the right paths throughout their lives. They will always have help on the journey of their vocation toward the goal of heaven. We are all called to be saints, and like children, we do best when we have a good example to follow.

. . . .

There is a moment in the Mass during the Liturgy of the Eucharist when we pray the Sanctus, or the "Holy, Holy, Holy." It is a moment when we "join with the angels and saints to sing of our salvation." The angels and saints are constantly praising God in heaven, and here we do the same. Though he wasn't speaking about the Mass, C. S. Lewis wrote that "the Present is the point at which time touches eternity."[11] The Sanctus is a profound moment in which we can be close to the saints and actively worship with them.

I learned this only about a week before we lost Ethan, in reading *The Lamb's Supper* by Scott Hahn. I marvel now at the way God put those words into my line of vision and let me take them in just then. Weeks later, I remembered them, and daily Mass meant even more to me than it had before. Physically Ethan's not with us, but in that moment, we are all together in the way I pray we will be at the end of days.

Parenting is a messy business, and there's a lot of room for doubt. The culture tells us that your best is good enough and don't forget to consider yourself and your needs too. The Church tells us, love yourself, yes, but love your Lord above all else. It is possible to raise saints, to become saints ourselves, if our eyes and hearts are pointed in the right direction.

When caring for four immortal souls feels overwhelming, I look to St. Thérèse of Lisieux's family. If anything about them seems old-fashioned, consider that her mother's lace business was so successful, her father ended his watch business to help her with hers. And all this while losing four children and raising the five who survived to adulthood to be religious sisters. It is no wonder that Zélie and Louis Martin were canonized together, as a couple. Marriage is sanctifying. Family life is sanctifying. This vocation to which I am called is the path to sainthood, if I ask for help along the way.

The saints are people who have strived for perfection and often relied on saints before them to do the same. They knew they couldn't live their vocations on their own, and at a pivotal moment in their lives, different for each of them, they stopped trying.

The saints are nuns, monks, priests, and popes. They are single people. They are children. They are parents. They are our brothers and sisters. They are our help.

• • • • • • • • • • • • • • • • • • • •

REFLECT

- What benefit do you see in asking a friend here on earth to pray for you when you're struggling with something? How do you respond when someone asks for your prayers?
- Where is an area in your life that you could use a friend to offer wisdom or guidance? Is there a particular saint you feel drawn to?
- To which saint might you entrust each of your children? Share the stories of these saints with your family.

• • • • • • • • • • • • • • • • • • • •

PRAY

Dear Lord, Father of us all, you give us the Communion of Saints to be our guides and cheerleaders in this world. Help us to look to their example and see sainthood as a real possibility in our lives. Help us to know we were never meant to run this race alone.

●●●●●●●●●●●●●●●●●●●●

CALL ON THE COMMUNION OF SAINTS

There are thousands of saints recognized by the Catholic Church, but there are countless faithful individuals who have not undergone the diligent and intense process of canonization. All these are our brothers and sisters in Christ who want nothing more than to pray for us so that at the end of time, we can all be together with our Father in heaven.

All you holy men and women, pray for us!

FIFTEEN

ON GIVING THANKS

DON'T FORGET TO SAY "THANK YOU"

One of the first phrases we taught our children in sign language was "thank you." Even when our culture can't agree on what's good and evil, saying "thank you" is considered basic human decency. Consider in how many languages you know the word for it, even if you don't know any more than that. *Merci. Gracias. Danke. Grazie.* In American Sign Language, the gesture is the fingertips touched to the chin and then the hand moved away from the face, as if blowing a kiss. It's a recognition of the kindness of another, a way to express gratitude for a gift given.

In my life, I've had a great deal to be grateful for, even if I haven't been able to see it right away. For one thing, I always knew the opportunities I had to go to college and travel abroad were gifts. What I didn't expect was that seeing more of the world would help me be grateful for the beauty of what "home" means to me.

I spent a lot of time traveling my junior year of college. I went on a service mission trip to Belize, came home to work at a bookstore for a while, and then spent a semester in Berlin, Germany, during which I also traveled to England, Ireland, and

France. John and I had been together for three years, and we talked often and openly about marriage at some point after we graduated. Still, I expected I would come home from these trips ready for more travel, based on the experiences of those who went before me. I was excited, and I anticipated that seeing so much more of the world would compel me to spend more time exploring the planet.

In Belize, we visited alumnae from our school who were serving a two-year term in the Jesuit Volunteer Corps. I think most of us pictured ourselves in their shoes. I know I did. Volunteering after graduation was a popular thing to do on my undergraduate campus, even before the financial crisis of '08. I figured it would take some explaining to my parents and maybe even to John, but I knew if I felt the call, if I got fired up, I'd have to go. Personally, I welcomed the challenge.

The work we did in Belize was powerful. We ran a camp for schoolchildren in Punta Gorda before traveling to Belize City, where we were to build a house for a small family. It was a square of something like sixteen by sixteen feet, roughly the size of one of our common rooms back at school.

Early in the week, our work came to a halt due to a lumber shortage. Thursday we learned that the family we'd come to know—the grandmother, Louise, who shared a name with my own mother; her husband, who showed us how to hack open a coconut and drink the water inside; and their granddaughter Sheryl, whom my teacher-in-training friend confided in me was woefully behind in her development—did not own the land on which they resided. The people who did own it did not want a house on it.

We were in a collective state of shock: humbled, pained, and confused. We said a Rosary together. We then asked the priest who had traveled with us to celebrate Mass. It was the only thing we could figure to do.

Later, we tearfully loaded the base we'd built onto a truck and drove it across town to the next family on the list. We didn't have time to meet them, but we were assured that they really did own their tract of land. Before we knew it, it was time for us to go home.

Things were very different in Germany. I shared an apartment with a forty-year-old artist. Every day I saw remnants of the division between East and West that had ended when I was too little to understand it. I rode freely through the Brandenburg Gate on my bicycle whenever I liked. I was living in a place rife with twentieth-century history and was regularly in awe of it, of the triumph of good in this place that had been blanketed with evil. At the same time, I was learning how to live on my own, to use a language that was not my native tongue, and to fill my days with things that were meaningful to me.

The hardest day of the semester was a Sunday. I didn't have schoolwork to do. My roommate and the friend I'd traveled overseas with were busy. I had nothing to do, but not in a good way. I felt displaced, distanced from the city I was smack in the middle of. I was incredibly lonely. I rode my bike around, but all I could see were the people eating al fresco with family and friends, enjoying each other's company. I considered seeing a movie, but there wasn't anything I wanted to see, all by myself in a dark room. I might have read, but I couldn't concentrate. I felt alone.

I turned to prayer, but I didn't receive immediate consolation. To be honest, I don't remember how I passed the rest of that day. I didn't have another day that tough the whole semester, even when I found myself unoccupied again. For whatever reason, it was that one that challenged me, and it was that one that taught me the greatest lesson I learned that year. It wasn't German grammar or history. It wasn't how to behave in another culture. Those things are important, sure. They're not quite as important, though, as being grateful for every single day of my life. That day, I had no choice but to lean on the Lord. I literally had nothing else in the whole world to do.

I came home not wanting to travel more, at least not immediately. I wanted to be at home, but not because of a fear of being lonely again. I wanted to be near my family because that's where I felt as if I fit, where I belonged. I was starting to recognize my vocation, the way God was calling me to love my neighbor and to draw closer to him. I knew with certainty that I wanted to be, forever, with John. Preparing to promise my entire life to one person and accept that children may soon follow was not what the majority of my peers were doing as we approached our senior year of college and readied ourselves to launch into the world. But I had a newfound gratitude for the gift of my relationship with John and for the direction I could see my life taking. This was where I was supposed to be. I didn't want to lose that. I also knew that I wanted a parish to be the main part of the community I lived and served in. This is where I felt most at home, where I felt my gifts could be used to serve.

I told John later that I would have been okay with him proposing the instant I was back in the States, I was so sure that our lives were meant to be shared so fully. We got engaged only nine months later and married eighteen months after that. On the weekend of our wedding, many of our friends said that at twenty-three or twenty-four, just a year out of school, they weren't anywhere near ready for marriage. Our friends were unanimous, however, that it made sense for us. They commented that during the wedding Mass, John and I recited our vows with steady voices. Neither of us cried, and our voices didn't waver. It was the next logical step for both of us. We knew we didn't know what was ahead, but we were committed to weathering it, laughing through it, and praying for it together.

I didn't expect that a mission trip and a semester abroad would give me such confidence in my vocation. I welcomed the challenge, and I was open to the possibilities of what the next few years would hold, wherever on the globe God called me. He called me home. He called me to people who love, challenge, and encourage me, who inspire me to grow in holiness, and who make me laugh my head off. He led me to people who didn't yet exist but whom I need as much as they need me.

Three of our kids are verbal now. Folks at church have commented on how polite they are (most of the time). They say "thank you" a lot, because they hear it a lot at home. Sometimes it's in jest, as in, "Thank you, love, for taking out that bag of garbage that's just sitting by the front door because it's freezing out and I don't want to go." Most of the time, it's sincere: "Thank you for doing the dishes tonight so I could finish this article." "Thank you for enduring these pregnancies." "Thank you for checking in with me midday to see how I was doing."

John is good about thanking God for the good and the bad at the end of the day, reminding the kids and me that everything is an opportunity to grow closer to our Lord, as long as we've got the eyes to see it. The more grateful we are, the more we see. The more we see, the more grateful we become for the ways God moves in our lives.

Every day if I can manage it, I give thanks to God in the context of the Holy Mass. *Eucharist* means "thanksgiving" and as such is a necessary element of my relationship with God my Father, who has given me my life, my family, and my vocation.

Mass is the ultimate prayer experience. Even with squirmy babies who "need my blanket, Mom!" "want snack cup!" or "want to go home!" it is just plain good for us. I receive many of the graces I need to live my motherhood well by virtue of being present at Mass and participating as best I can: a plea for forgiveness, thanks for the blessings and challenges set before me, and food for the journey to which I return.

Taking little ones to Mass every day is a challenge, and not because it's early in the morning. We're typically up two hours before Mass begins in these parts. But the reason we're there is more than logistics. For John and me, in living out the promises we made at our children's Baptisms, the Mass is critical. We vowed to lead our children in the faith, to be their first teachers. In our own promises, renewed each year at least at Easter, if not more often, we profess our belief in God, our rejection of Satan, and our faith in the Church. Our relationship with God is the most important thing in our lives. We choose to put it at the center. We choose to give thanks. It is certainly right and just to do so.

. . . .

REFLECT

- How often do you express gratitude to the people in your life, in both the major and minor things?
- Is there anything in your life you're not grateful for? Why not?
- Think back to a time in your life when you were angry or hurt, especially if you had difficulty forgiving in that

situation. Where can you find something to be grateful for in it?

• • • • • • • • • • • • • • • • • • • •

PRAY

Thank you, Father, for your many gifts, especially those I haven't yet recognized for what they are. Increase my appreciation for your love of me, just as I am, today, right now, and help me to pay that generosity forward to everyone I interact with today.

• • • • • • • • • • • • • • • • • • •

CALL ON THE COMMUNION OF SAINTS

Once he stopped persecuting Jesus, St. Paul committed his life to spreading the Gospel and sharing the love that had changed his life. A tremendous missionary and apostle, St. Paul writes in his first letter to the Thessalonians, "Pray without ceasing. In all circumstances give thanks, for this is the will of God for you in Christ Jesus" (1 Thes 5:17–18). We must always pray; we must always be grateful. This is the only way to truly, deeply know and love our Lord.

St. Paul, pray for us!

EPILOGUE

I AM SO PROUD OF YOU

Growing up, I understood that my parents were more concerned with the effort I put into things than with the results. I was often told to try my best and that my best would be enough.

So it is in our relationship with God, except that as Christians, we have a secret weapon: grace. Our Father knows that we can't do it on our own and that trying our best really means surrendering the circumstances of our life to him. His goal for us is not to gain prestige in this world but to enter heaven, where we will enjoy eternal life. We can't achieve that without his help. We need mercy and grace; we need Jesus, our brother and our Lord, the perfect example of love in its most diligent and expressive form.

I live with the hope that at the end of my days on earth, God will look upon me and say, "Well done, my beloved daughter. I am pleased with you." My vocation as a mother is the path by which I am to travel toward this ultimate goal. I am charged with giving my best, with the understanding that my "best" means giving it all up to him. It means recognizing God's role in my life, his providence and his will.

As a mother and as God's daughter, I need to work hard, discipline myself, and serve in little ways with my whole heart. But with the stresses of contemporary life, even these seemingly simple resolutions and knowing that I'm not asked to do it all can feel overwhelming. Just trying to love in every circumstance is tough. It's not what the rest of the world suggests, for sure.

It's then that I recall how I feel about my own children. I love them simply for who they are, no matter what they do. I want them to try their best, but I know there will be moments when, for a variety of reasons, they can't or won't. In these times, I will do my best to correct them, to encourage them in a way that will positively motivate them. But it will not change how deeply I love them. It will not change their worth in my eyes.

I value my children immensely; I would sacrifice myself for them as Jesus did for me. I am proud of them for being the amazing, unique, beautiful gifts they are. Sometimes it is enough to just listen to them laugh to take my breath away in wonder and delight. So it is with God my Father for me, his beloved daughter.

There are a lot of forces in the world saying that I am not enough. I am not supposed to need anyone else—no rules to follow, no standards to uphold. Supposedly, I can choose what's right for me, what matters, and what has value. This, somehow, will lead to me having everything I want—not necessarily everything I need.

God my Father knows more about me, his daughter, than I know about my children. He knows not only the hairs on my head but also the thoughts that inspire me, the feelings that compel me. He wants to see me succeed, and he wants me to call on him when I need him. He wants me to bring my will to him and lay it at his feet, taking up his instead. As a daughter of God, baptized and adopted into this family, I have a calling, a vocation, and it is to my earthly family, to my husband, children, parents, in-laws, community, and the people my children bring into my life simply by course of their existence. I am made richer by being a mother. I am made more whole.

Thank God for this vocation of motherhood. It is a constant and obvious call to sacrifice my will to that of another. It forces me to ask questions about the faith and formulate answers profound but simple enough that, literally, a child could understand them. It makes me like a child myself, reaching for someone to guide me and trusting in someone with greater wisdom who can show me what it really means to love.

Most people would agree that at the end of our lives, the parts we will be most proud of will be our children. Should it be any different with God when we reach the end of our lives?

Sometimes I think that the goal of raising my children, apart from their reaching heaven, is that when they are grown, they will want to come home again. Not to live, not to rely on John and me to continue to support them, except in extreme circumstances, but to visit, to enjoy our company, and to revel in the love they experienced by being one of our children, our beloved sons and daughters, and people we see ourselves in but who are so much more. Our children are gifts, unique and individual.

I have a tradition of writing my children letters. They don't know this, and I don't intend for them to see them until they are at least eighteen. I write about what I've seen and learned as they grow. Sometimes I write about tough things we faced, and I assure them that we did the best we could. I want them to understand where they came from, to see me as a human, fallible, who tried her best. I hope these letters will give them courage as adults, and maybe as parents, to try their best, to not be afraid to fail, and thus to become more fully the people God intended them to be.

In my oldest child's letters, there is a theme of a particular gratitude. It is this child who made me a mother. By no choice of his own, he gave me the gift of starting on the journey of my vocation. I couldn't do it without him, you might say. When we clash heads, it's most often the result of a behavior or tendency we have in common. It's something of myself that I see in him, and I want so badly to show him how to do it right, even though it's a struggle for me.

Mothering him and his siblings is the most joyful, challenging, exhausting, exhilarating, and sometimes stinky job I've ever had. It may be cliché, but there's truth in this saying: my children are my greatest treasure, and I am so, so proud of them.

At the end of our lives, may God our Father say the same of us.

RECOMMENDED READING

Often, the books I enjoy reading the most and that are the most fruitful for my mind and soul are those recommended to me by people I love and trust. If this book has inspired or encouraged you, I hope you will pass it on to someone you think will benefit from it. In the meantime, I'd like to share a couple of books from my shelf—in addition to those I've referred to or cited in the prior sections of this book—that I come back to time and again.

John Bergsma. *Bible Basics for Catholics: A New Picture of Salvation History.* Notre Dame, IN: Ave Maria Press, 2015.

Who said illustrated books were only for kids? A professor at the Franciscan University of Steubenville uses line drawings to bring home his pared-down exploration of salvation history. Those who have yet to experience a solid Catholic Bible study will find a good foundation here. Dr. Bergsma has similar books on the New Testament and the book of Psalms as well.

Jeff Cavins. The Great Adventure Catholic Bible Study series. Necedah, WI: Ascension Press. biblestudyforcatholics.com.

Speaking of Catholic Bible studies, this one is incredible. I started with *A Quick Journey through the Bible* (2007), which culls a linear timeline from the breadth of the seventy-three books of the Catholic Bible. Cavins's style is erudite but accessible. Prepare to be amazed at connections you'd never realized before; suddenly, seemingly esoteric Mass readings have context! The basic understanding he offers was a large part of his coming into the Catholic Church, and his love for our faith is contagious.

Michael Gaitley. *33 Days to Morning Glory: A Do-It-Yourself Retreat in Preparation for Marian Consecration.* Stockbridge, MA: Marian Press, 2013 (available via Ignatius Press).

It is difficult to put into the words the change I experienced when I first consecrated myself to Mary: an increased sense of peace, trust, joy, and comfort. This book guided me as I prepared, encouraging me with stories of Sts. Louis de Montfort, Maximilian Kolbe, Teresa of Calcutta, and John Paul II. Each day's reading is brief and builds on the prior day's. I love that there is a chart with suggestions for when to begin so that you end on a Marian feast day. "To Jesus through Mary!"

Scott Hahn and Kimberly Hahn. *Rome Sweet Home: Our Journey to Catholicism.* San Francisco: Ignatius Press, 1993.

I love reading conversion stories. I've been drawn back and deeper into the faith at various stages of my life for a bunch of different reasons. It always affirms and inspires me to see what about the Catholic Church and its teachings draws others out of the ways of the world and into a fuller, more complete life. The Hahns' story is a testament to the power of prayer and the sacraments as well as a celebration of marriage.

C. S. Lewis. The Chronicles of Narnia. 7 books. London: HarperCollins, 2013.

I couldn't get into these books as I child, but I adore them as an adult. The connections to the spiritual life resonate with me every time. I use them as teachable moments with my kids when I can. I'm also left with a deeper desire to seek the Lord and engage in real prayer when story time is over. Bonus: Because they're written for children, you can get through them quickly!

C. S. Lewis. *Mere Christianity*. New York: HarperOne, 2012.

Forgive my double dose of Lewis—I love the guy. It took me a while to muster the courage to dive into this book, despite it being on my to-read list for ages. When I did, I was surprised (in a good way) to find that the book is a collection of radio talks Lewis gave between 1941 and 1944, explaining Christianity in a way the masses—still reeling from the Great War—could relate to. The chapters are accessible, honest, and straightforward. If you weren't convinced of the reality and necessity of Christ before, you will be.

Kate Wicker. *Getting Past Perfect: How to Find Joy and Grace in the Messiness of Motherhood*. Notre Dame, IN: Ave Maria Press, 2017.

Every woman of our time needs to read this book. With humor and honesty, Wicker navigates the reality of being a mother in the twenty-first century. We face unique challenges that require unique solutions, but it all comes back to the ever-lasting, unstoppable, unconditional love of our God. We are perfect when we live to be the women God made us to be.

NOTES

1. John Paul II, "Address of John Paul II to the Young People," Auckland, New Zealand, November 22, 1986, http://w2.vatican.va/content/john-paul-ii/en/speeches/1986/november/documents/hf_jp-ii_spe_19861122_giovani-auckland-nuova-zelanda.html.

2. Anne-Marie Slaughter, "Why Women Still Can't Have It All," *Atlantic*, July/August 2012, https://www.theatlantic.com/magazine/archive/2012/07why-women-still-cant-have-it-all/309020.

3. Henri J. M. Nouwen, *A Spirituality of Waiting: Being Alert to God's Presence in Our Lives* (Notre Dame, IN: Ave Maria Press, 2006), audio edition.

4. St. Ignatius of Loyola, "Suscipe," accessed July 19, 2017, https://jesuitprayer.org/prayer-of-st-ignatius-suscipe.

5. Hal Hingdon, "Marathon Training Guide: Novice 1," accessed May 13 2017, http://www.halhigdon.com/training/51137/Marathon-Novice-1-Training-Program.

6. Nouwen, *Spirituality of Waiting*.

7. Nouwen, *Spirituality of Waiting*.

8. Pedro Arrupe, "Falling in Love with God," in *What Are We? An Introduction to Boston College and Its Jesuit and Catholic*

Tradition (Chestnut Hill, MA: Center for Ignatian Spirituality, Boston College, 2002), 94.

9. Michael Erard, "Escaping One's Own Shadow," *Opinionator* (blog), *New York Times*, September 29, 2012, https://opinionator.blogs.nytimes.com/2012/09/29/escaping-ones-own-shadow-in-writing/?emc=eta1.

10. Adam Grant, *Originals: How Non-Conformists Move the World* (New York: Viking, 2016), 166–67.

11. C. S. Lewis, *The Screwtape Letters* (1942; repr. New York: HarperCollins, 2001), 75.

LINDSAY SCHLEGEL is a freelance writer and editor and a regular contributor to *Verily* magazine and *CatholicMom.com*. She served in various roles in the book publishing industry for more than a decade.

Schlegel earned a bachelor's degree in English and German from Boston College in 2008. She lives with her family in northern New Jersey.

www.lindsayschlegel.com

DANIELLE BEAN is the brand manager at *CatholicMom.com*.

CATHOLICMOM.COM BOOKS

The CatholicMom.com Books series
addresses issues women in all stages
of life care about most—
faith, family, work, and relationships—
from a uniquely Catholic perspective.
Building on the popularity
of the award-winning *CatholicMom.com*
website, as well as founder
Lisa M. Hendey's books
The Handbook for Catholic Moms
and *A Book of Saints for Catholic Moms*,
the series is written by trusted
CatholicMom.com contributors
and other Catholic authors
who are deeply committed
to their faith and families.
CatholicMom.com is a ministry
of Holy Cross Family Ministries,
which, like Ave Maria Press,
is an apostolate of the Congregation
of Holy Cross, United States
Province of Priests and Brothers.

**Find all the books in the series
at avemariapress.com.**